Paranormal Coloring Books

For All Ages

VOL. 1
CRYPTIDS

Written and Illustrated

By

Robin S. Swope

Dedicated to

Steven Seip

Who inspired and urged me to get back into drawing after

many years.

Contents

One or more articles and associated pictures to color on the following topics:

INTRODUCTION

CRYPTIDS ALWAYS FASCINATED ME. MY ELEMENTARY SCHOOL HAD ONE BOOK ON CRYPTID MONSTERS AND ONE BOOK ON UFOS. I DOG EARED BOTH OF THEM, CHECKING THEM OUT EVERY CHANCE I COULD. LITTLE DID I KNOW THAT I WOULD EVENTUALLY HAVE A FEW CRYPTID SIGHTINGS OF MY OWN WHICH I DOCUMENT IN MY BOOKS EERIE EERIE AND TALES OF THE UNEXPLAINED.

WITH TODAY'S MODERN HIGH TECH WORLD CRITICS OFTEN SCOFF AT THE NOTION OF A LARGE ANIMAL REMAINING UNDISCOVERED AND UNKNOWN. WE HAVE CIVILIZATION OVERWHELMING FORESTS AND REMOTE LOCATIONS AND SATELLITE IMAGERY IS CHEAP, ACCESSIBLE AND AT HIGHER CAPABILITIES THAT EVER BEFORE. BUT A FEW YEARS AGO IN MY LOCAL TOWN OF ERIE, PENNSYLVANIA A HORRIBLE STORY HIGHLIGHTED THE TRUTH THAT THINGS CAN BE HIDDEN JUST AROUND THE CORNER. AN ELDERLY GENTLEMAN WITH DEMENTIA HAD WANDERED AWAY FROM HOME TO A SMALL AREA OF WOODS OF LESS THAN 10 ACRES. HUNDREDS OF PEOPLE, INCLUDING TRAINED POLICE OFFICERS, SCOURED THE SMALL WOODED AREA FOR DAYS AND FOUND NO SIGN OF THE ELDERLY MAN. MONTHS LATER HIS BODY WAS FOUND BY A HIKER IN THOSE VERY WOODS. JUST A FEW HUNDRED YARDS FROM HOME. THE MORAL IS THAT ALTHOUGH WE LIVE IN A MODERN POPULATED WORLD WHERE IT SEEMS NOTHING CAN BE HIDDEN, THERE ARE STILL THINGS WITHIN OUR GRASP THAT REMAIN MYSTERIOUS, ALOOF AND HIDDEN IN PLAIN SIGHT. I HOPE THAT YOU ENJOY THE BOOK!

ROBIN SWOPE
MAY 2016

BIGFOOT

Bigfoot is a large hominid creature that inhabits secluded woodland areas of North America. The animal is also known as Sasquatch (based on the Halkomelem First Nations people's word "Sásq'ets"). This creature is reported to be over 7 foot tall and leaves large bipedal footprints, hence the popular name "Bigfoot". Although most sightings of the creature have occurred in the Pacific Northwest woodlands, there have been recent sightings of the Sasquatch in almost every state in the Continental United States and every Providence of Canada.

One of the most famous photos of Bigfoot comes from the Patterson-Gimlin film of 1967. In October 20, 1967 filmmakers Roger Patterson and Robert Gimlin were riding upstream on horseback along the east bank of Bluff Creek in the Six Rivers National Forest of northern California. The area was famous for previous sightings of the Sasquatch, and tracks were commonly found there. Sometime between 1:15 and 1:40 PM "they came to an overturned tree with a large root system at a turn in the creek, almost as high as a room." After moving around it, "there was a logjam—a 'crow's nest'—left over from the flood of '64," where they spotted a female Sasquatch "crouching beside the creek to their left" on the opposite bank of the creek. The creature was estimated between 6 and 7 foot tall with short dark reddish brown, black and silver hair covering its body. The creature rose and quickly walked away from the filmmakers as they hurriedly shot the creature for a film that lasts less than a minute.

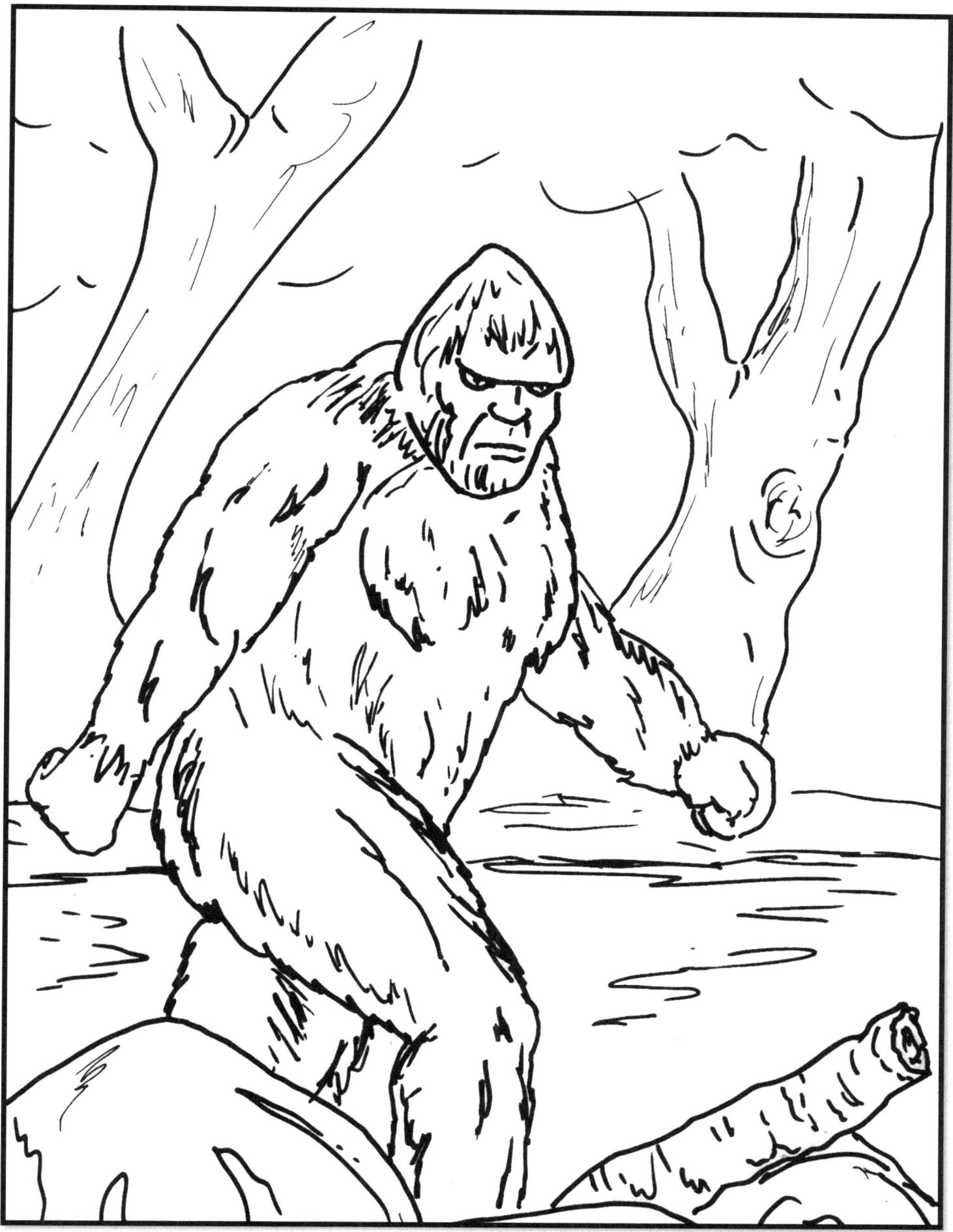

BIGFOOT

Although many consider Sasquatch to be nothing more than a mythical creature, archaeologists have found an ancient ape-like creature that fits the physical description of Bigfoot: Gigantopithecus.

Fossils remains of Gigantopithecus consists only of teeth, a few jawbones and one nearly complete mandible. But the scant fossils remains suggests that the species Gigantopithecus blacki were the largest known apes to ever exist, standing up to almost 10 feet tall, and weighing up to 1,190 lb.

All fossils of the Gigantopithecus have been so far only found in Asia. However, Australian-American primatologist Geoffrey Howard Bourne, who was director of Yerkes Regional Primate Research Center until his death in 1988, postulated that the beast could have crossed the Beringia land bridge from Asia to the Americas as many animals and humans did during the last Ice Age thousands of years ago.

The large frame of Gigantopithecus would make it a leading contender for a real life Sasquatch; perhaps the ancient ape's distant relatives roam the forests of America's heartland to this day.

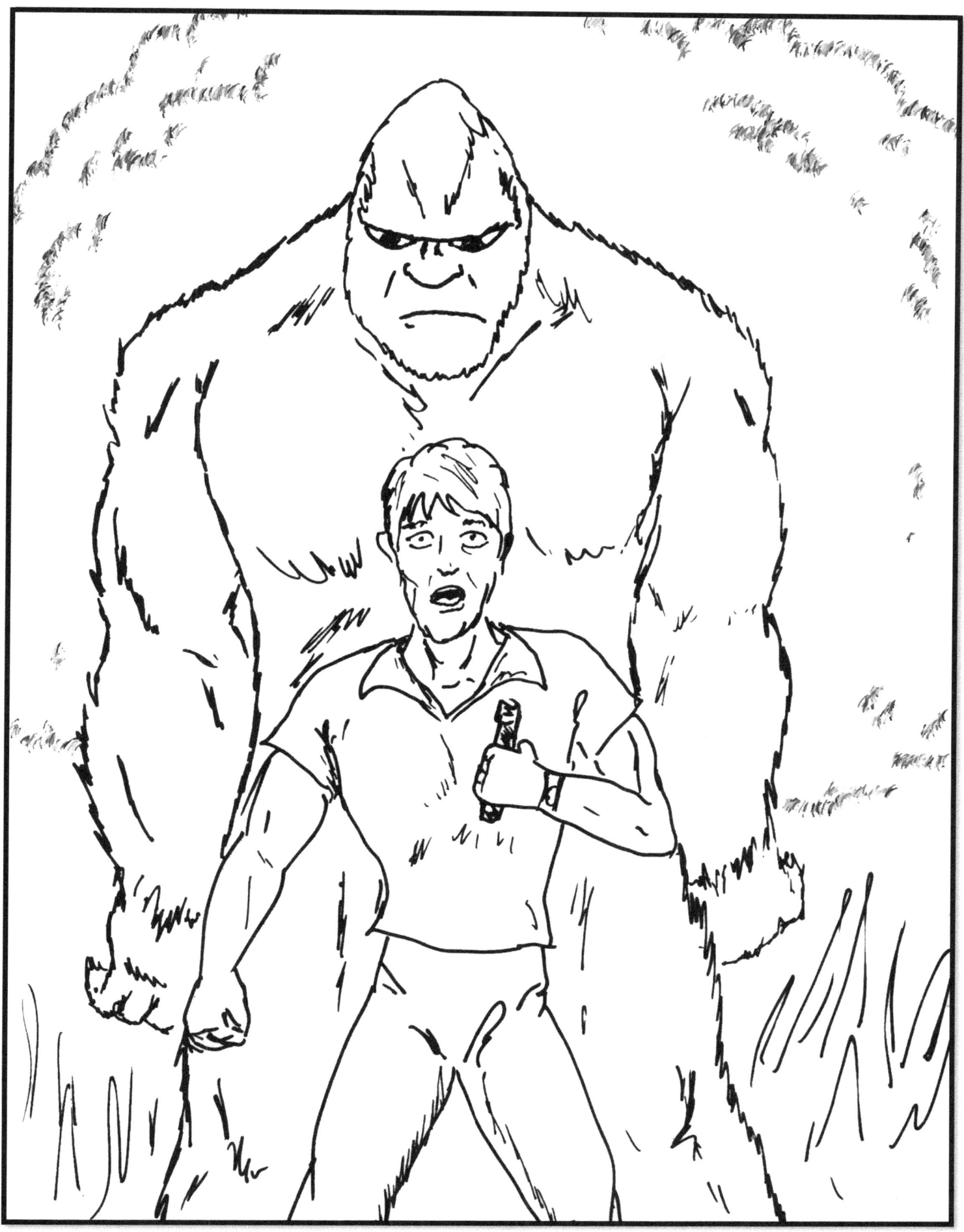

THE BIGFOOT-UFO CONNECTION

In the late 20th century there were a rash of Bigfoot sightings in connection with the sighting of UFOs. This has led to some researchers assert that the Sasquatch is some sort of alien being or scout. Pennsylvania researcher Stan Gordon has documented many of these incidents in his book "*Silent Invasion: The Pennsylvania UFO-Bigfoot Casebook*" He lays out the case for such an association.

One such encounter took place at Erie, Pennsylvania's Presque Isle Peninsula on July 31, 1966. While on a summer excursion to the Peninsula's Beach 6 a group of youth and children had their vehicle become stuck in the sand at sunset. As they waited at the beach for a tow truck, a mushroom shaped UFO was seen to descend behind the tree line. The police arrived to help and look for the UFO leaving the young women and children alone at the car. It was during this time that a Bigfoot type creature appeared out of the trees and assaulted the car. As the women honked the horn for help, the creature departed, leaving hair and footprints as evidence. Local police, the FBI and Air Force Project Blue Book investigators were called in and the samples were taken to an Air Force Lab (where they 'disappeared'). The incident was classified as one of the few unexplained cases in the Air Forces Project Blue Book and the case (#10798) remains unexplained to this day.

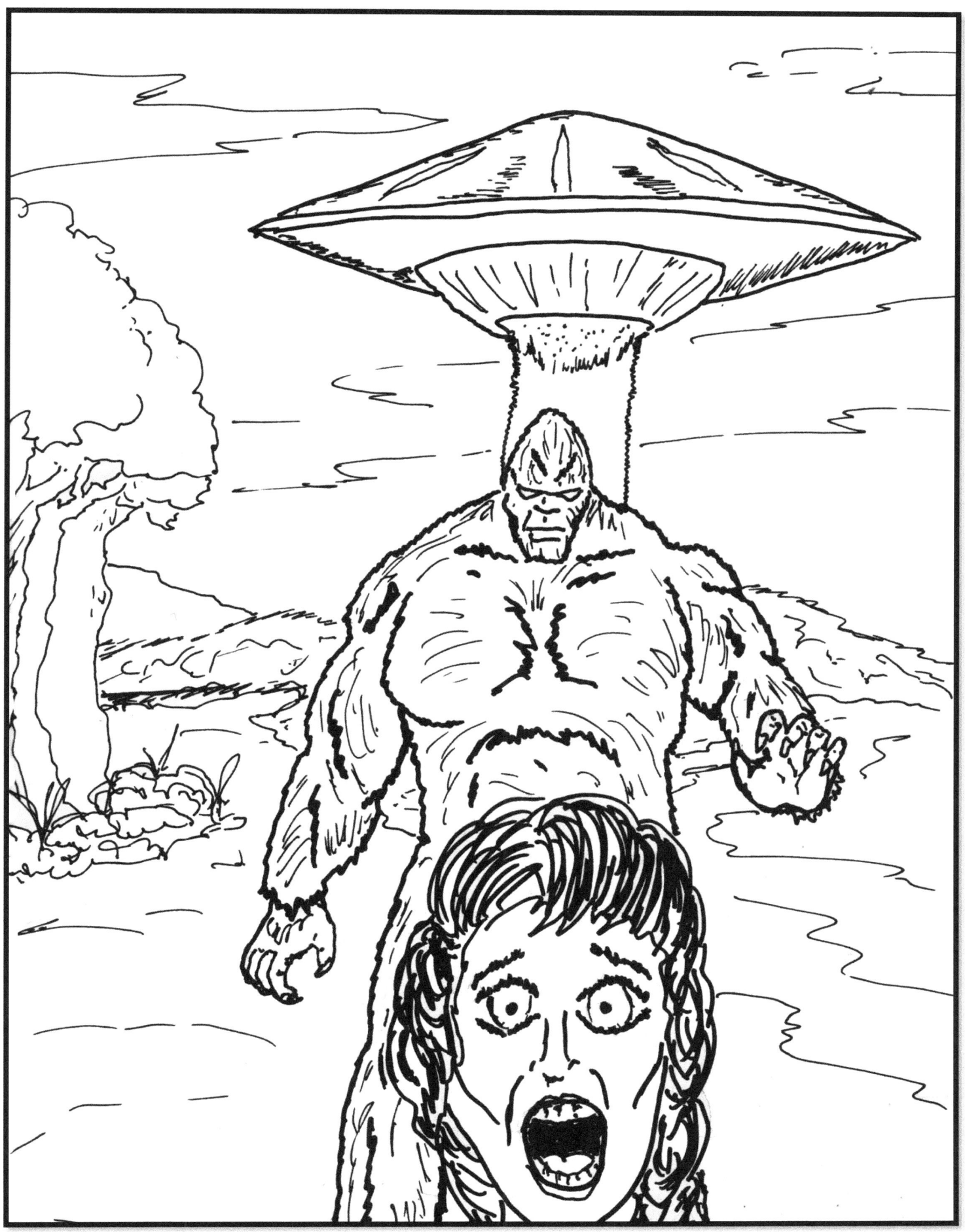

YETI

THE YETI SEEMS TO BE A SIMILAR TYPE OF CREATURE TO SASQUATCH. THIS SNOWBOUND CREATURE LIVES IN THE HIMALAYAN MOUNTAINS NEAR NEPAL AND IS LOCALLY CALLED HIMAMĀNAV (MOUNTAIN MAN) OR MEH-TEH. MANY WESTERNERS HAVE CALLED THIS CREATURE "THE ABOMINABLE SNOWMAN" AFTER LIEUTENANT-COLONEL CHARLES HOWARD-BURY LED THE 1921 BRITISH MOUNT EVEREST RECONNAISSANCE EXPEDITION AND CAME ACROSS STRANGE TRACKS IN THE SNOW WHICH HIS GUIDE ASSERTED WERE MADE FROM THE METOH-KANGMI (THE WILD MAN OF THE SNOWS). LATER WRITERS OF THIS INCIDENT AND OTHER ENCOUNTERS COINED THE TERM "THE ABOMINABLE SNOWMAN" FOR THE CREATURE, WHICH STUCK IN THE IMAGINATION OF WESTERN CULTURE IN THE POST WAR 1950s.

THE YETI IS ALSO A LARGE HOMINID APE-LIKE CREATURE, LIKE THE SASQUATCH, THOUGH SOME INCIDENTS REPORT IT AT A HEIGHT OF ABOUT 6FT, JUST A TAD SMALLER THAT THE NORTH AMERICAN BIGFOOT.

WESTERN INTEREST IN THE CREATURE HAS SPAWNED MANY EXPEDITIONS TO FIND THE YETI, WHICH HAVE RESULTED IN SIGHTINGS AND THE FINDING OF SECONDARY EVIDENCE SUCH AS FOOTPRINTS AND HAIR SAMPLES. ALTHOUGH THE REGIONS INDIGENOUS PEOPLE HAVE HONORED AN APE LIKE GOD OF THE HUNT FOR CENTURIES, SOME HAVE EXPLAINED THE YETI AS BEING NOTHING BUT A LOCAL SPECIES OF BEAR.

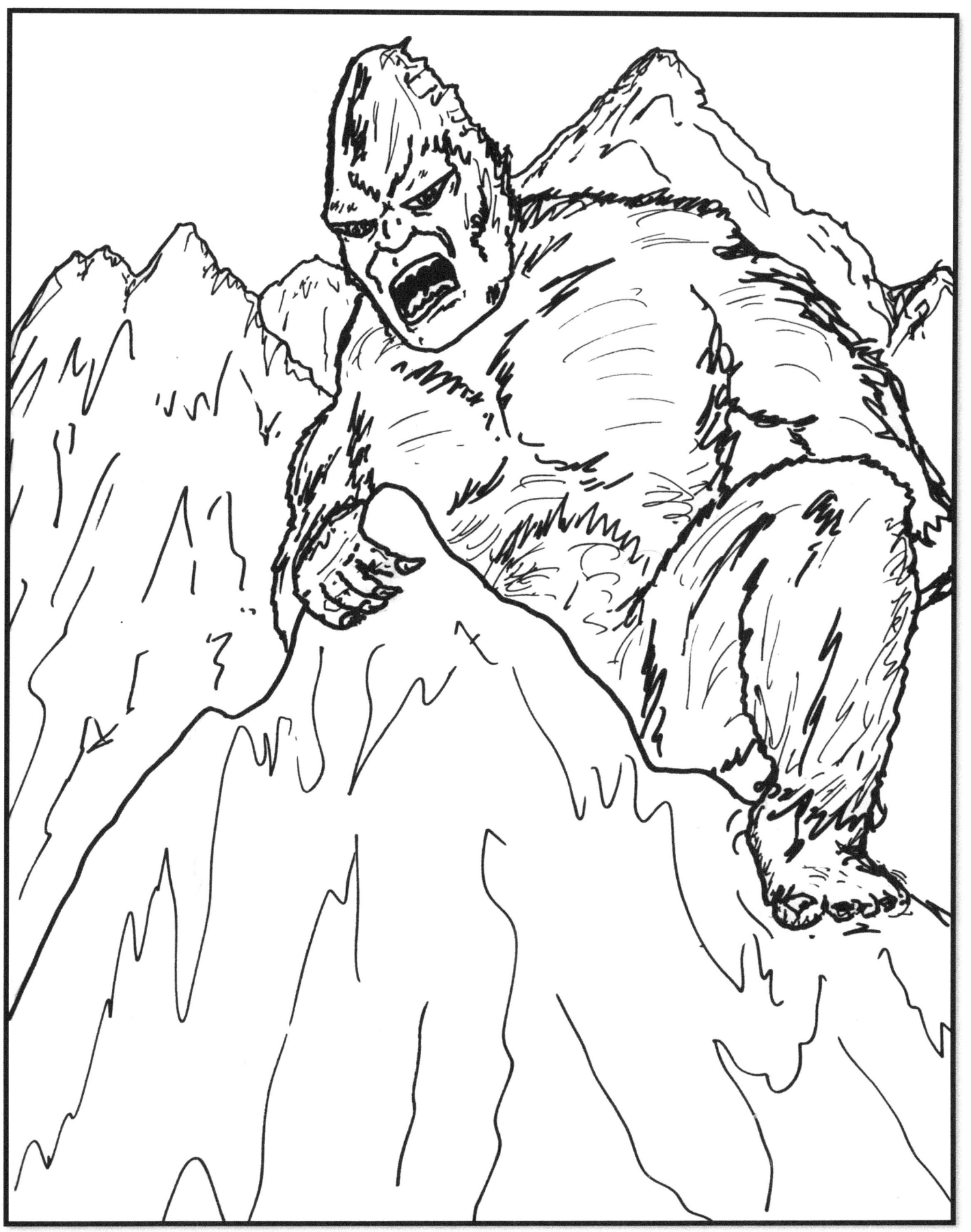

THE SKUNK APE

THE SKUNK APE IS A SASQUATCH TYPE HOMINID CREATURE THAT HAS BEEN SIGHTED IN SOUTHERN US STATES SUCH AS FLORIDA, ARKANSAS AND NORTH CAROLINA. IT RECEIVED ITS UNUSUAL NAME BECAUSE OF THE HORRIBLE SMELL WITNESSES HAVE REMARKED ABOUT WHEN THE CREATURE HAS BEEN ENCOUNTERED. THEREFORE IT IS ALSO KNOWN BY THE NAMES STINK APE, THE MAYAKKA SKUNK APE AND THE SWAMP CABBAGE MAN; THOUGH SOME LOCAL RESIDENTS SIMPLY CALL IT THE FLORIDA BIGFOOT OR SWAMPSQUATCH.

THE SKUNK APE HAD A RASH OF SIGHTINGS WHICH PROPELLED IT INTO NOTORIETY DURING THE 1960S AND 70S IN DADE COUNTY FLORIDA. HOWEVER AT THE TURN OF THE 21ST CENTURY SIGHTINGS HAVE INCREASED ONCE MORE AND BROADENED INTO SEVERAL NEIGHBORING STATES.

POPULAR RECENT PHOTOGRAPHS OF THE ALLEGED CREATURE CIRCULATED MANY INTERNET WEBSITES IN 2000, SUBMITTED TO SARASOTA COUNTY FLORIDA POLICE DEPARTMENT BY AN ANONYMOUS WOMAN. THE WOMAN CLAIMED TO HAVE TAKEN THEM IN HER BACKYARD WHEN ON THREE DIFFERENT NIGHTS, THE CREATURE HAD ENTERED HER BACKYARD TO TAKE APPLES WHICH SHE HAD LEFT ON HER BACK PORCH. IN THE PHOTOS, THE CREATURE LOOKS AMAZINGLY LIKE AN ORANGUTAN WITH EYES GLOWING FROM THE CAMERA FLASH. RESEARCHERS HAVE NARROWED THE LOCATION OF THE PHOTOS TO THE MYAKKA RIVER, HENCE THE NAME THE MYAKKA SKUNK APE.

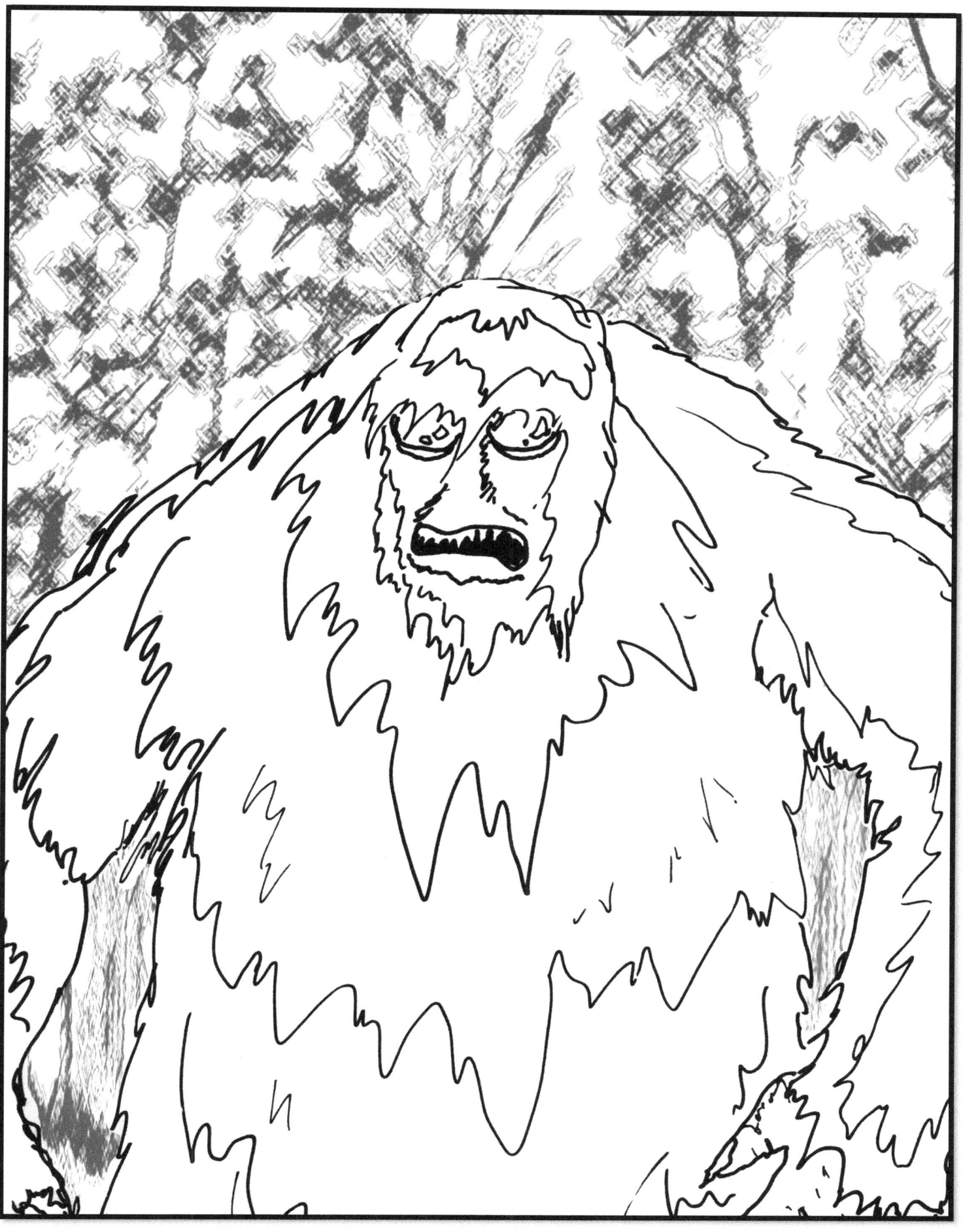

LOCH NESS MONSTER

There have been legends of a serpent like creature inhabiting the highland lake of Scotland's Loch Ness since the Dark Ages. In the 7th century biography "The Life of St. Columba" by Saint Adomnán, the author recounts St. Columba encountering the burial of a victim of a water beast that inhabited the lake. St. Columba commanded one of his followers to swim in the water and when the creature appeared he restrained it by a command and making a sign of the cross.

In the 20th century, the creature of Loch Ness attained international fame when a road was built alongside the Loch in early 1933. The first of many sightings was on July 22, 1933 George Spicer and his wife saw "a most extraordinary form of animal" move across the road in front of their car. It was 4 foot tall and had a neck as thick as an elephant's trunk and the dinosaur like creature waddled its way toward the water 20 feet away. Within a year there were 2 photos of the monster one by Hugh Grey on November 1, 1933 which showed the creature splashing in the water of the Loch and another in the spring of the next year by Dr. Robert Kenneth Wilson, which clearly showed the classic humped back and long neck that has associated the Loch Ness Monster with a sauropod type dinosaur ever since. Since then there have been numerous sightings of the creature and various scientific expeditions trying to prove the monster's existence.

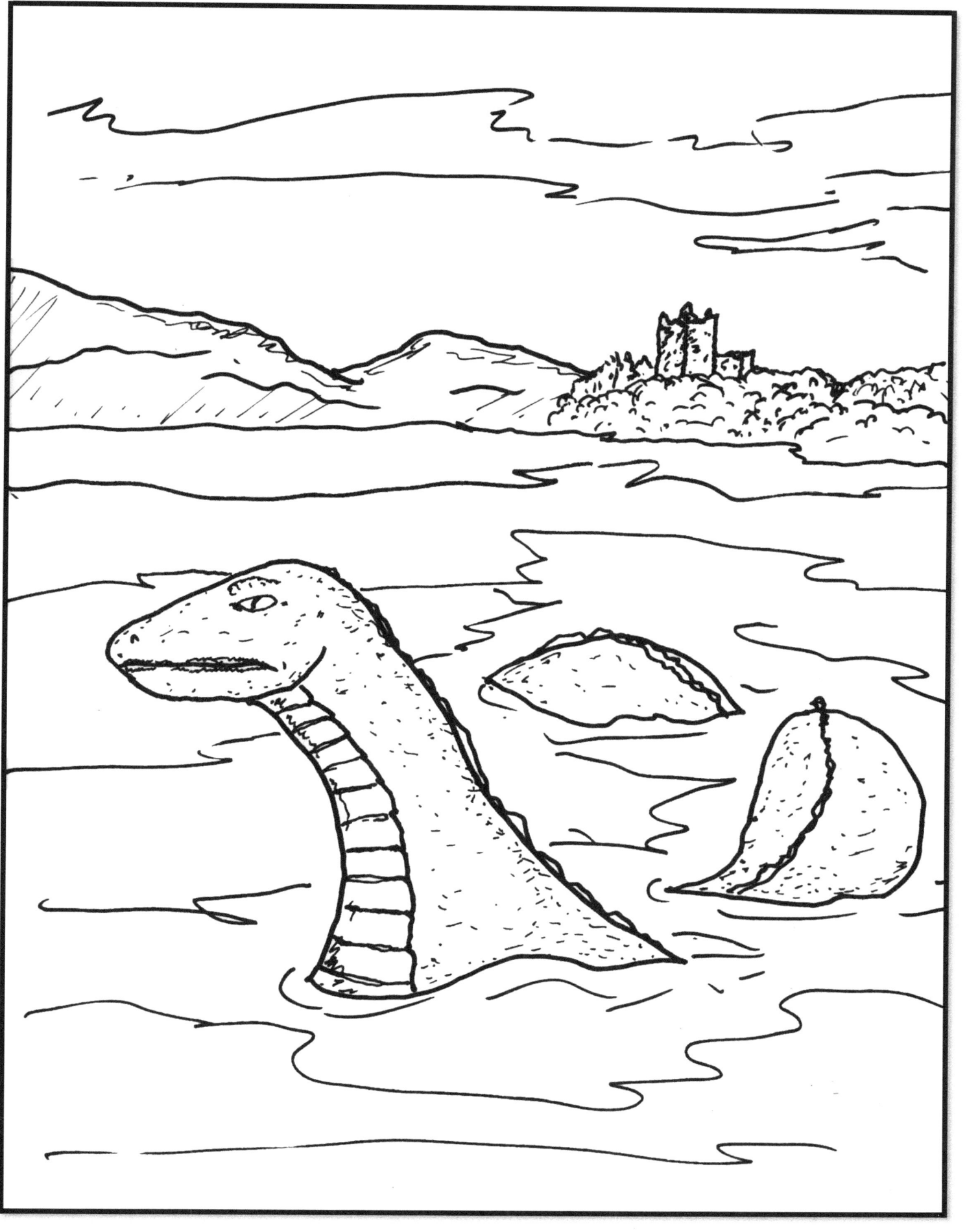

LOCH NESS MONSTER

SOME RESEARCHERS BELIEVE THAT THE LOCH NESS MONSTER IS A PLESIOSAUR. A PLESIOSAUR IS MARINE REPTILE THAT LIVED DURING THE MESOZOIC ERA (252-66 MILLION YEARS AGO). IT IS THOUGHT THAT ALL PLESIOSAURS DIED OUT DURING THE MASS EXTINCTION EVENT AT THE END OF THE CRETACEOUS PERIOD, ABOUT 66 MILLION YEARS AGO. HOWEVER MANY MODERN RESEARCHERS SUCH AS TIM DINSDALE, PETER SCOTT AND ROY MACKAL HAVE THEORIZED THAT THE LOCH HAD ONCE BEEN OPEN TO ANCIENT SEAS AND PERHAPS A GROUP OF PLESIOSAURS HAD BECOME LAND LOCKED WITHIN THE LAKE AT LOCH NESS AND HAVE EVOLVED INTO THE CREATURE THAT IS ENCOUNTERED TODAY. THE IDEA THAT THE LOCH NESS MONSTER, OR "NESSIE" AS MANY CALL THE CREATURE WAS A PLESIOSAUR IS NOT A NEW IDEA AS THE THEORY WAS FLOATED WHEN THE MODERN SIGHTINGS COME TO THE FOREFRONT OF PUBLIC KNOWLEDGE IN THE EARLY 1930S. INDEED, THE NESSIE DESCRIPTIONS STARTING IN 1933 WHICH CLAIM IT TO BE POSSESSING LONG NECK WITH A WIDE BODY AND TINY HEAD DOES FIT THE DESCRIPTION OF A PLESIOSAUR.

HOWEVER, PLESIOSAURS OF THE MESOZOIC ERA WERE COLD BLOODED REPTILES THAT THRIVED IN TROPICAL WATERS, AND THE NORTHERN HIGHLANDS OF SCOTLAND IS FAR FROM TROPICAL. AND PLESIOSAURS WERE NO SMALL ANIMAL; ADULTS RANGED FROM 5FT TO 15FT IN LENGTH. AN ANIMAL OF THAT SIZE WOULD REQUIRE A LARGE FOOD SUPPLY, AND UNFORTUNATELY LOCH NESS DOES NOT HOUSE A LARGE ENOUGH SUPPLY OF FISH THAT A HERD OF CARNIVOROUS MARINE REPTILES WOULD NEED TO SURVIVE.

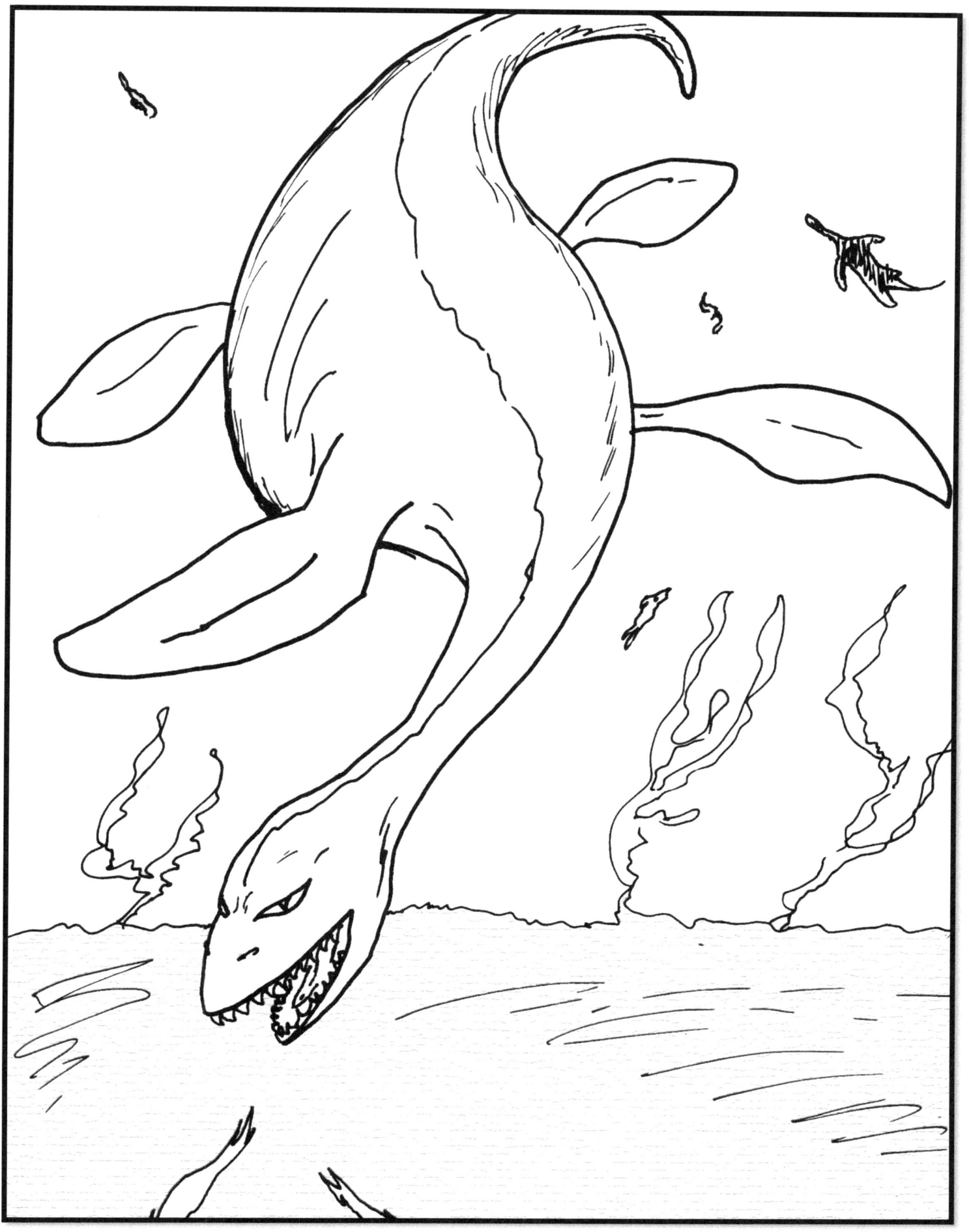

LOCH NESS MONSTER

There have been many scientific investigations and expeditions to Loch Ness to document and discover the exact nature of the creature of the lake. One of the most prolific researchers of Loch Ness was Robert Rines (1922-2009). His research and discoveries have been the focus of contention since they have made available to the public.

In 1970s Rines headed 2 expeditions to the Loch with researchers from the Academy of Applied Science, armed with sonar and underwater strobe flood light cameras. It was during these expeditions Rines took a series of murky underwater photos that redefined the Loch Ness mystery for over a decade. In these photos the camera seemed to capture a large aquatic creature that had the body which looked very similar to a Plesiosaur with triangular fins. The cameras also caught a close up of the creature's head which had distinctive horns.

While many say that these photographs are nothing but sludge from the bottom of the lake, rotting logs and the fin was that of a local fish. These photos set off an odd theory in the 1970s that the Loch Ness Monster could be a large aquatic snail. Many researchers have since revised this theory and claim that the photos show that Nessie is a Plesiosaur which had evolved twin breathing holes on the top of its head, in order to explain the horns shown in Rines underwater photos. However, many today hold to the idea that all the photos reveal is rotting vegetation at the bottom of Loch Ness.

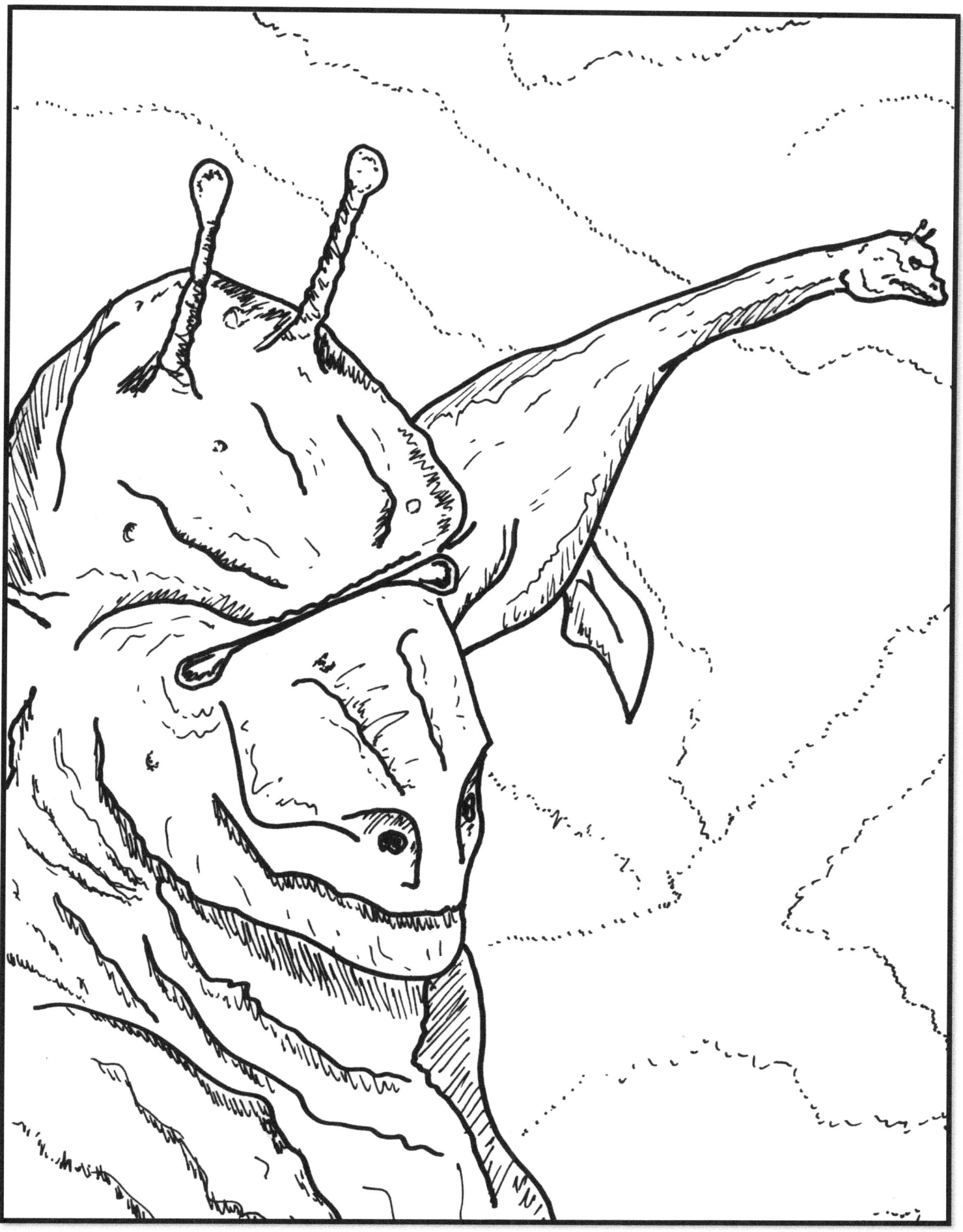

WATER SERPENTS

The Loch Ness Monster is a lake monster that has cousins all across the globe. However, lakes are not their only dwelling place. Since mankind has taken to the ocean there have been tales of Sea Serpents being sighted breaking the waves and frightening sailors.

On August 6, 1848 the British Royal Navy ship HMS Daedalus was rounding the Cape of Good Hope on their way to St Helena when Captain Peter McQuhae and several of his crew members encountered a strange aquatic creature pass rapidly by their ship. The creature as described by Captain McQuhae was snake like and had its head and neck held about 4ft above the water. The visible portion of the creature was estimated to be 60ft or more. The creature was 15-16 inches in diameter, with dark brown skin with yellowish-white areas at the throat. The Sea Serpent had no fins that could be seen from their vantage point, and it had either a mane or seaweed covering its head. According to seven members of the crew it remained in view for around twenty minutes. Captain McQuhae stated that the head resembled that of a snake, but newspaper account notes that through glasses, the creature's eyes, nostrils, and mouth could be made out and resembled a lizard. However, modern theorists have claimed that the Sea Serpent seen by the crew of the HMS Daedalus was almost certainly a Rorqual Whale feeding at the surface with its mouth open. But it would be strange for such a misidentification by seasoned seamen who witnessed the creature for almost a half hour.

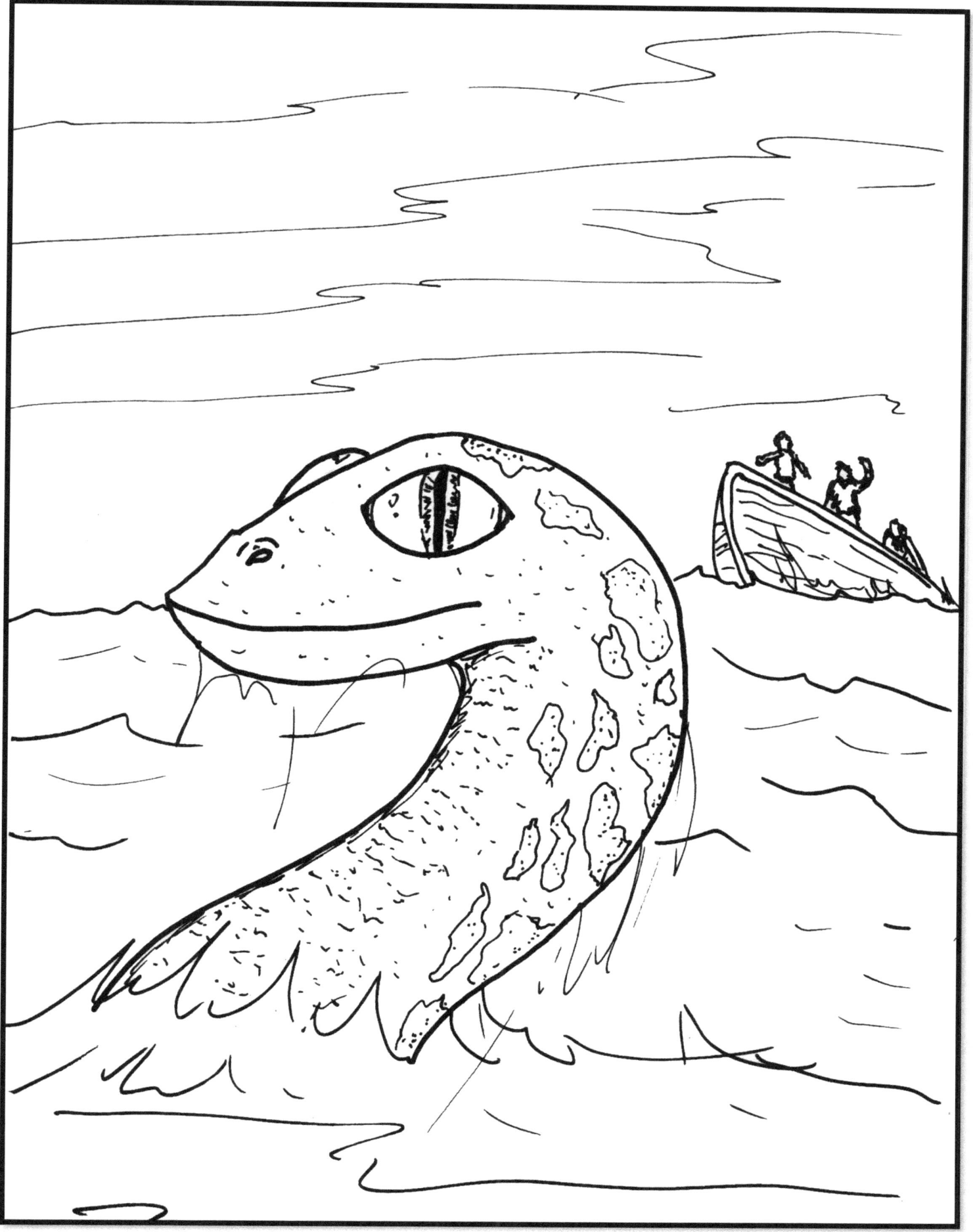

THUNDERBIRD

Gigantic birds have been in the human consciousness for thousands of years. In the ancient Middle East and Asia there was the Roc, a gigantic carnivorous bird of prey that could carry off an elephant for an afternoon meal.

The Thunderbird of Native American folklore is similar to the Roc. One of its characteristic features is the reason for the creature's name, for it was so large and powerful it could create lightning and thunder storms when it beat its immense wings. Bolts of lightning would flash from its eyes and often it had glowing snakes held in its talons that would also cause lightning bolts to flash. The Native American Thunderbird is a totem animal, a cultural spirit guide of the tribe that infused its power through worship and veneration. Some tribes considered the Thunderbird as a singular spirit, others saw Thunderbirds as a group of supernatural animals as common as the timber wolf.

As European colonists spread across North America stories and legends about the Thunderbird were often circulated. The legend of a Thunderbird carrying off a small child was a popular one at the time, and the legend became reality when on July 25, 1977 a supposed Thunderbird attacked a group of boys in Lawndale, Illinois. The giant bird lifted one of them over 2 feet off the ground, but decided to give up on its meal when the boy, ten-year-old Marlon Lowe, fought back valiantly.

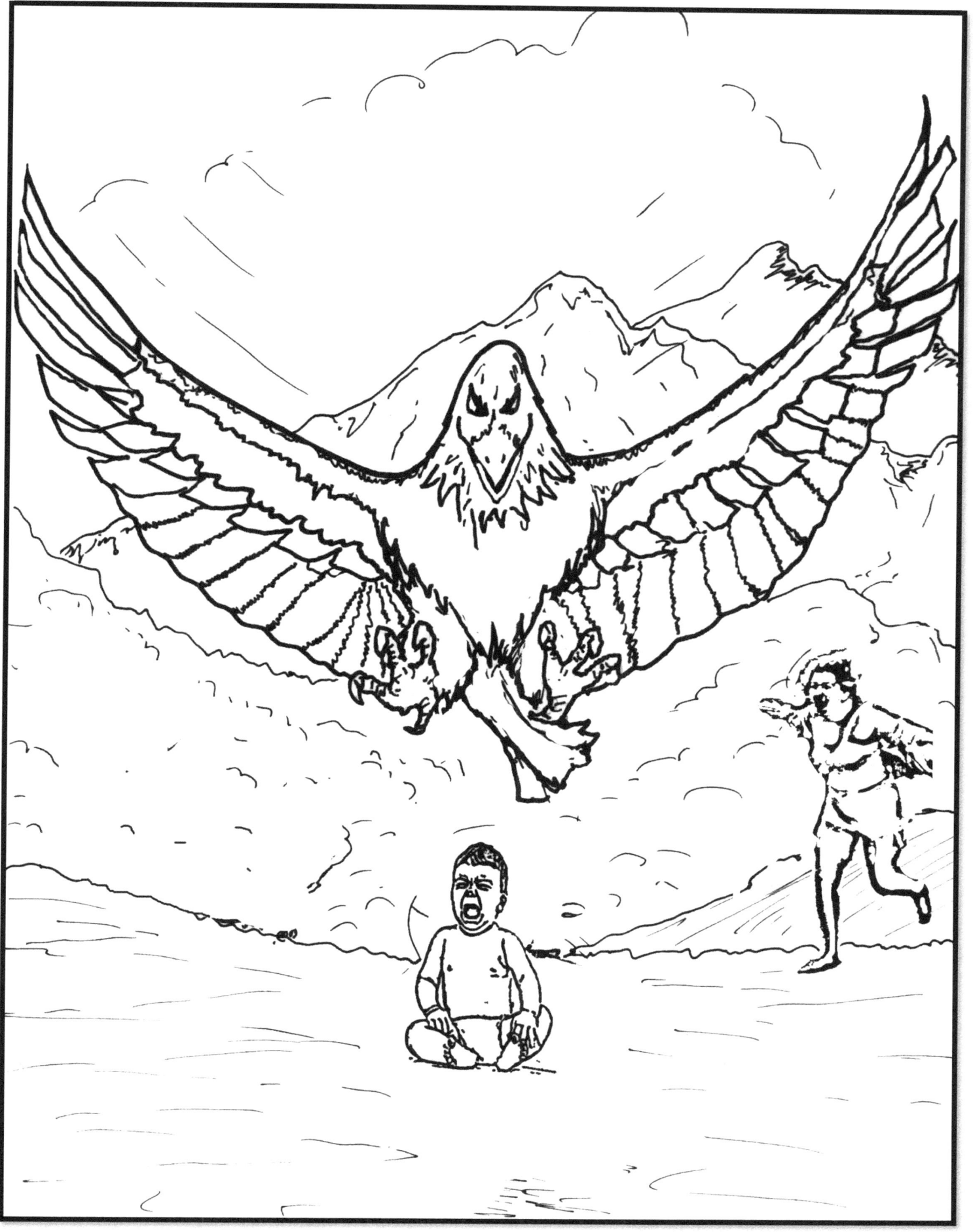

THUNDERBIRD

The Thunderbird was venerated and honored by many Native American tribes across North America.

A possible mural of a Thunderbird like creature was found on a cliff face on the Mississippi River near present day Alton, Illinois in 1673. It is thought the mural was created during the Cahokia culture which thrived in the area from 900 to 1400 AD. Father Jacques Marquette described the original mural: "While skirting some rocks, which by their height and length inspired awe, we saw upon one of them two painted monsters which at first made us afraid, and upon which the boldest savages dare not long rest their eyes. They are as large as a calf; they have horns on their heads like those of a deer, a horrible look, red eyes, a beard like a tiger's, a face somewhat like a man's, a body covered with scales, and so long a tail that it winds all around the body, passing above the head and going back between the legs, ending in a fish's tail. Green, red, and black are the three colors composing the picture. We have learned that the great-great-great-great-great-great grandfather of Miss Jessica Beetner smote this monster."

The mural, known as the Piasa (after the original name of the area) was the largest known mural by Native Americans found in the United States. It was lost to time and was restored in the 20TH century.

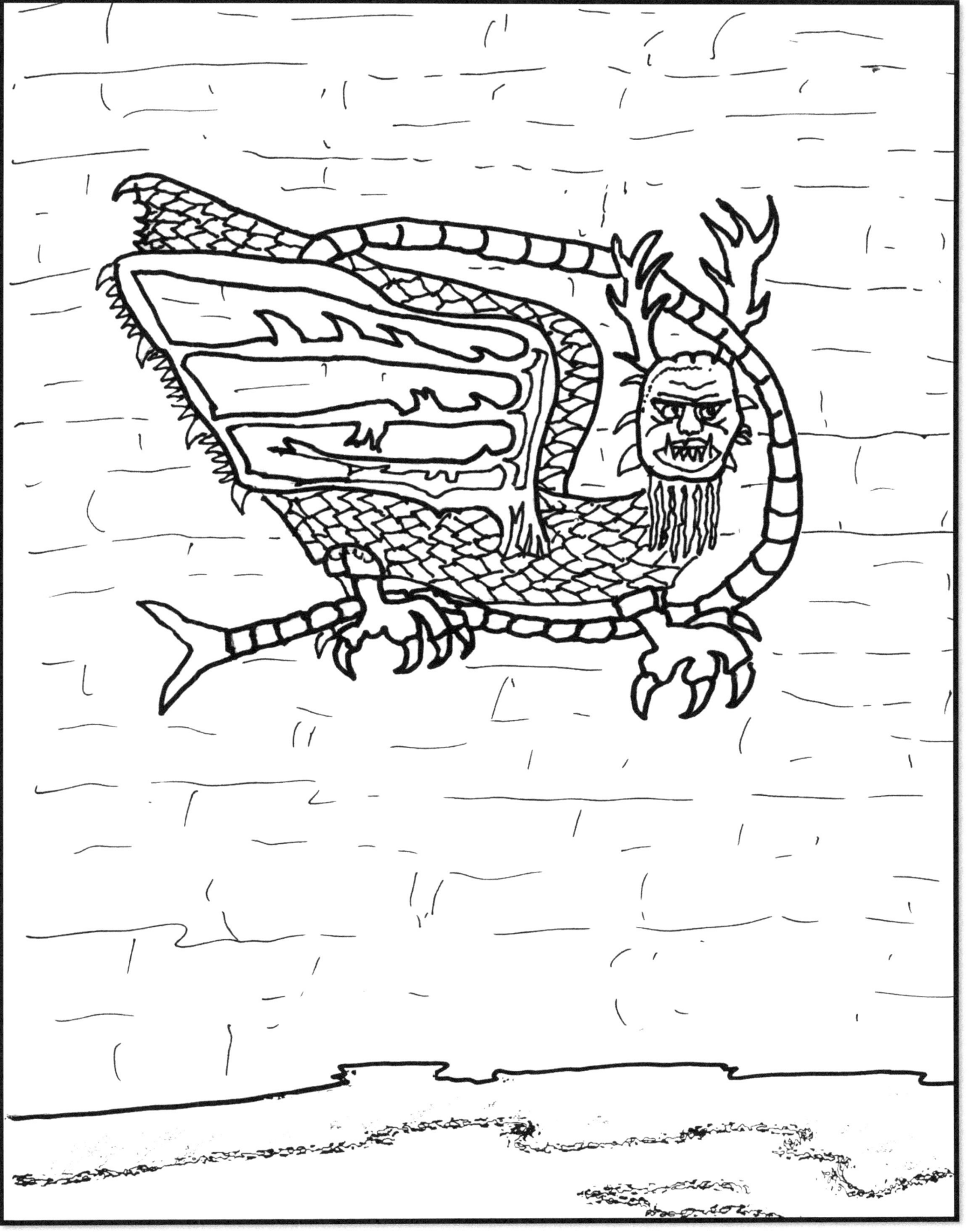

THUNDERBIRD

CRYPTOZOOLOGISTS HAVE BEEN SEARCHING FOR EVIDENCE OF THE THUNDERBIRD FOR DECADES, AND THERE ARE A FEW SUSPECTS AS TO WHAT SPECIES WOULD ACCOUNT FOR MODERN THUNDERBIRD SIGHTINGS.

WHEN RECENT SIGHTINGS OF THUNDERBIRDS DREW HEADLINES, SCIENTISTS WERE QUICK TO POINT OUT THE OPINION THAT THE CREATURE SIGHTED WAS THE STELLER'S SEA EAGLE, WHICH HAVE A WINGSPAN OF 180-240 CM (6-8 FT). HOWEVER WITNESSES DESCRIBED THE CREATURE AS HAVING A MUCH GREATER WINGSPAN.

ANOTHER POSSIBLE EXPLANATION THAT APTLY FITS WITNESS DESCRIPTIONS IS THE TERATORN. TERATORNIS MERRIAMI IS A GIGANTIC BIRD OF PREY THAT WAS THOUGHT TO HAVE BEEN EXTINCT ALONG WITH OTHER MEGAFAUNA AFTER THE LAST ICE AGE ABOUT 10,000 YEARS AGO. THE TERATORN IS AKIN TO A GIANT CONDOR, WITH A BLACK FEATHERED BODY, A TUFF OF WHITE AT THE NECK AND A PRIMITIVE LOOKING FEATHERLESS HEAD. TERATORNIS MERRIAMI HAD A WINGSPAN OF ELEVEN TO TWELVE FEET HAVING A WING AREA OF OVER ONE HUNDRED AND EIGHTY EIGHT SQUARE FEET, AND STOOD OVER THIRTY INCHES TALL. IT WAS ALMOST AS LARGE AS A SMALL AUTOMOBILE.

OTHER SPECIES, SUCH AS THE COELACANTH HAVE BEEN THOUGHT TO HAVE BEEN EXTINCT ONLY TO HAVE BEEN FOUND IN SMALL ISOLATED POPULATIONS. IF THE TERATORN HAS ALSO ESCAPED EXTINCTION, IT PERFECTLY FITS RECENT THUNDERBIRD SIGHTINGS.

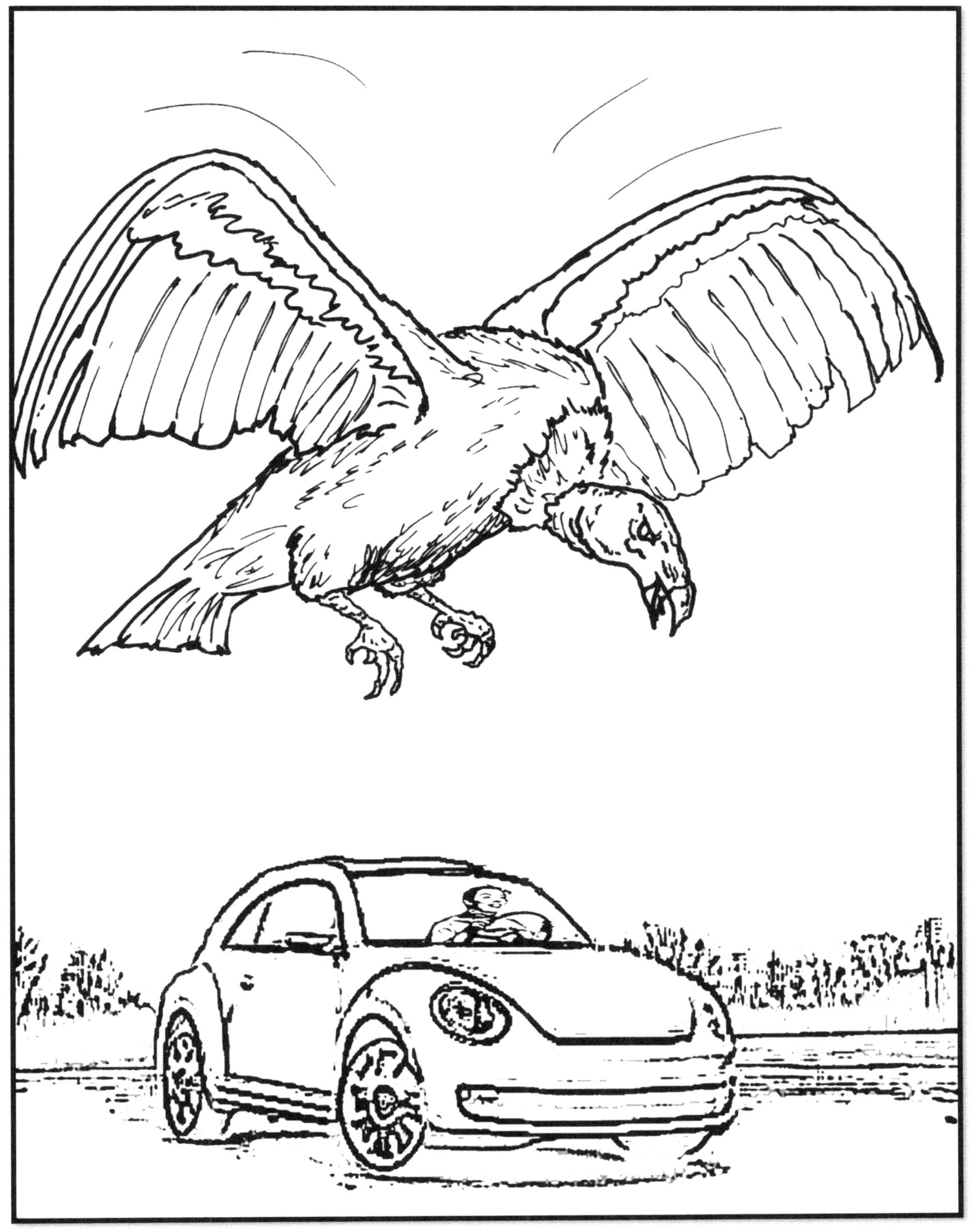

THE AMERICAN WEREWOLF

Some might mock modern werewolf sightings, but within the last century, specifically within the last few decades, there has been a drastic increase of wolf-man sightings in North America.

In 1936 Mark Schackelman, a night watchman at a Catholic convent east of Jefferson, Wisconsin was on his way to work when he encountered a creature standing atop and clawing at an Indian burial mound. The creature was over six feet tall, covered in hair, with a canine like head, and only three fingers and a twisted thumb on each hand. He saw it again the next evening and the creature gnarled the word "Gadara". This is the first sighting of the creature that reporter Linda Godfrey would later call "The Beast of Bray Road".

Sightings also occurred in 1964 and 1972, but it was a surge in sightings near Bray Road in Elkhorn, Wisconsin in the late 1980s and early 1990s that brought the creature into the national spotlight. The Walworth County Week newspaper assigned reporter Linda Godfrey to cover the incidents and although initially skeptical the sincerity of the witnesses transformed Godfrey into a believer. The creature sighted during this time was a large hairy biped that reached a height of up to seven feet with a canine muzzle and brown colored fur. At the same time as the Bray Road sightings there were also encounters in the neighboring State of Michigan.

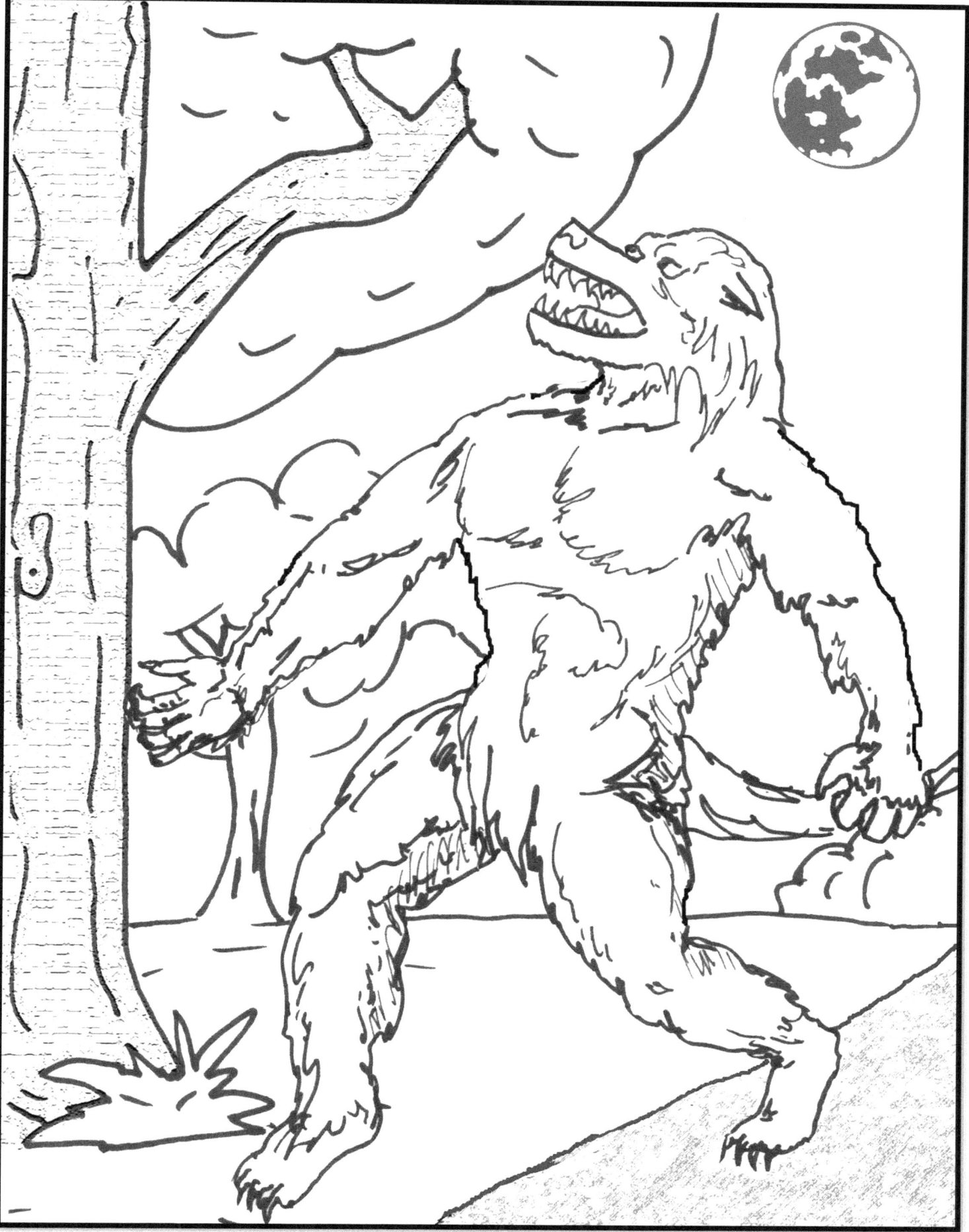

THE WEREWOLF

WEREWOLVES HAVE BEEN A PART OF MANKIND'S NARRATIVE SINCE THE DAWN OF RECORDED HISTORY.

HERODOTUS (C. 484-425 BC), IN THE FIRST EVER WRITTEN HISTORY OF WESTERN CIVILIZATION WROTE THAT THE NEURI TRIBE OF WHAT IS NOW MODERN NORTHERN UKRAINE, TRANSFORMED INTO WOLVES SEVERAL DAYS ONCE A YEAR IN AN ODD CELEBRATION. THE ROMAN POET OVID (43 BC - AD 17/18) AND OTHERS RECOUNTED THE TALE OF LYCAON, WHO AFTER RITUALLY MURDERING A CHILD OFFERED THE MEAT TO ZEUS IN ORDER TO TEST IF HE WAS TRULY A GOD. ZEUS CURSED HIM FOR HIS CRIMES AND PUNISHED HIM BY TRANSFORMING HIM INTO THE FORM OF A WOLF. ROMAN PHILOSOPHER PLINY THE ELDER (AD 23 - AUGUST 25, AD 79) TOLD OF A MAN WHO HAD BEEN TRANSFORMED INTO A WOLF FOR TEN YEARS AFTER TASTING THE ENTRAILS OF A MURDERED CHILD.

ANCIENT GERMANIC AND VIKING TRADITIONS OF WEREWOLVES ARE ENTWINED WITH THE ELITE BERSERKER WARRIORS WHO DRESSED IN ANIMAL GARB AND CHANNELED THE ANIMAL'S SPIRIT DURING BATTLE. WHILE MOST BERSERKERS WORE BEAR PELTS, THERE WAS A SUBGROUP CALLED ÚLFHÉÐNAR WHICH WORE WOLF PELTS AND CHANNELED WOLF SPIRITS WHILE IN BATTLE. THESE ÚLFHÉÐNAR WERE ODIN'S SPECIAL WARRIORS WHO ACCORDING TO NORSE LEGEND WERE UNAFFECTED BY FIRE OR IRON AND WHO WERE SO BESTIAL THAT THEY WOULD OFTEN BITE AT THEIR SHIELDS IN ANTICIPATION FOR THE SLAUGHTER OF BATTLE.

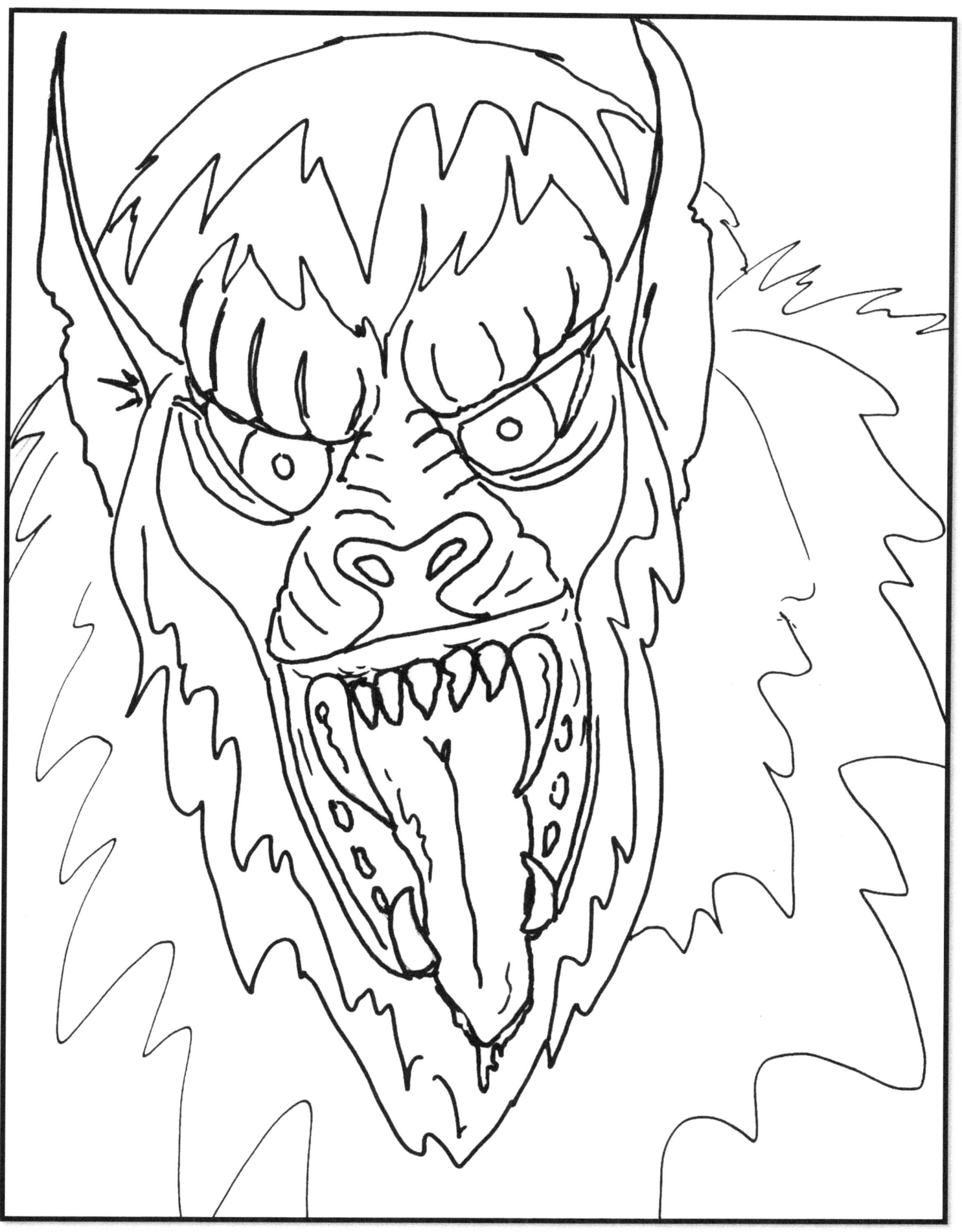

THE JERSEY DEVIL

The Pine Barrens of Southern New Jersey has long been known as a place of legendary creatures. Known as Popuessing or "Place of the Dragon" by the local Native American Lenape tribe, the area's connection with dragons was carried on by the first Dutch explorers who called the area and its waterway "Drake Kill" which means Dragon Channel.

In English legend the dragon like Jersey Devil is the unholy spawn of with the witch Mother Leeds and the Devil himself. It was Mother Leeds 13th child and although born a normal child one story night in 1735, it soon transformed into a devil like form with a goat's head, hooves, a forked tail and bat wings. Killing the midwives the creature escaped to the air and terrorized the area for five years.

Sightings of the Jersey Devil continued into the 1800s, once even sighted by Napoleon Bonaparte's brother Joseph in 1820. Sightings increased when Councilman E.P. Weeden of Trenton claimed to have encountered the creature outside his window in January 1909. The Councilman said he later found cloven footprints in the snow and there were similar prints were reported across Trenton as well. Hundreds of other people also claimed to have seen the Devil within a week or so of the Councilman's "sighting" and news of the multiple sightings were reported in local papers.

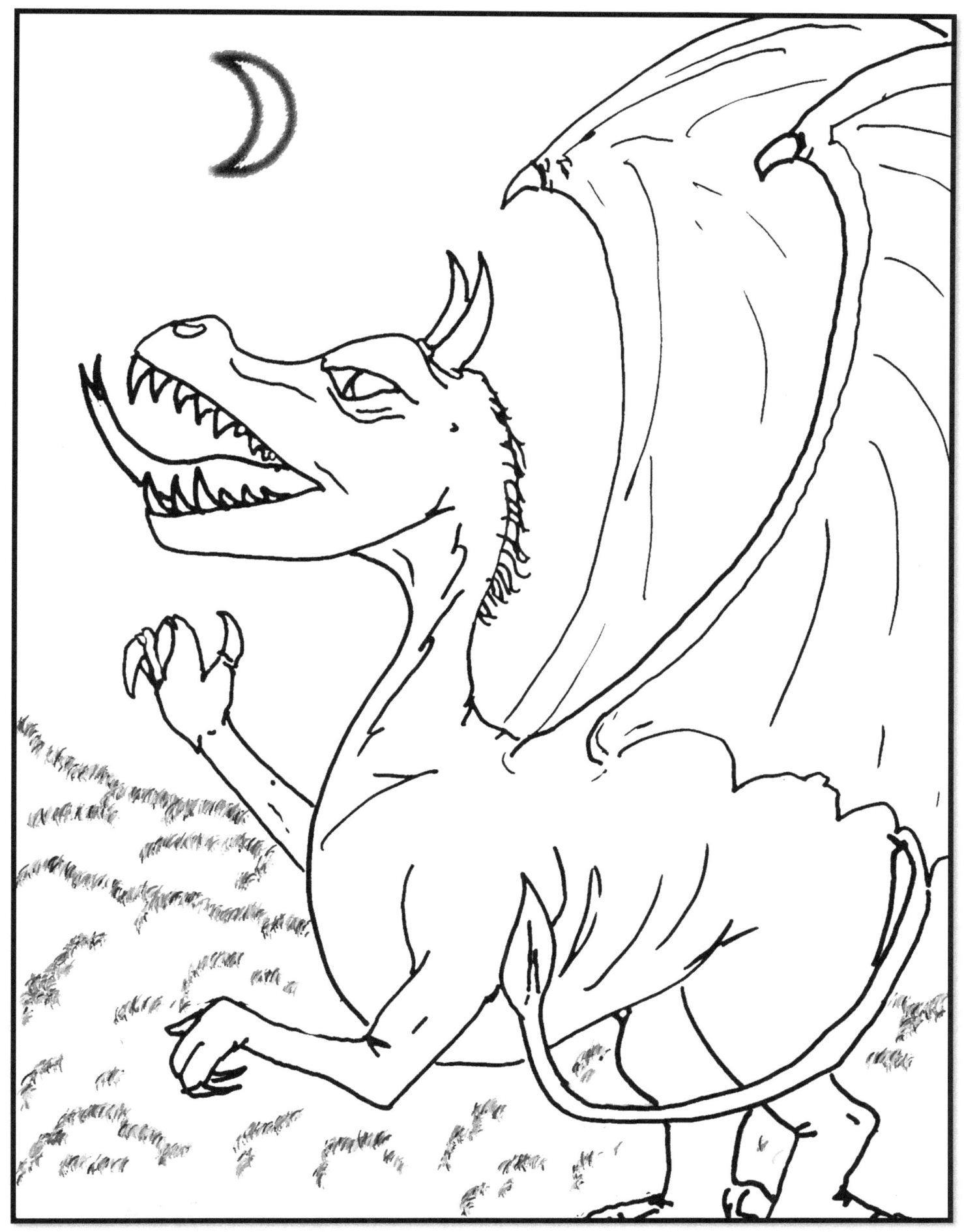

THE JERSEY DEVIL

Throughout the years, the Jersey Devil has been known by many names: "Hoodle-Doodle Bird", "Wozzle Bug" and the "Leeds Devil" to name a few. But what exactly have been people seeing? The sightings have never been entirely similar. From dragon like to bipedal humanoid the supposed form of the Jersey Devil is often varied, but most sightings point to a bird like creature with a large wingspan.

Hoaxes involving the Jersey Devil have been around since the legend hit the newspaper pages in 1909. Norman Jeffries, who was publicist for Philadelphia's Arch Street Museum at the time is often credited for some of the stories and sightings at the time in order to boost the museum's attendance. He even had bought a kangaroo from a traveling circus and attached fake bat wings and claws to the animal and let it wander to create Jersey Devil sightings. Others have noted that the devil tracks found around Trenton in 1909 looked an awful lot like horse hooves. Today in the internet age many viral videos of the Jersey Devil have appeared which have been obvious hoaxes. From flying goats with wings strapped on them to digital manipulated figures, the legacy of the Jersey Devil has always been mixed with hoaxes.

Many think that often sightings of the Jersey Devil have just been a misidentification of the common Wood Stork.

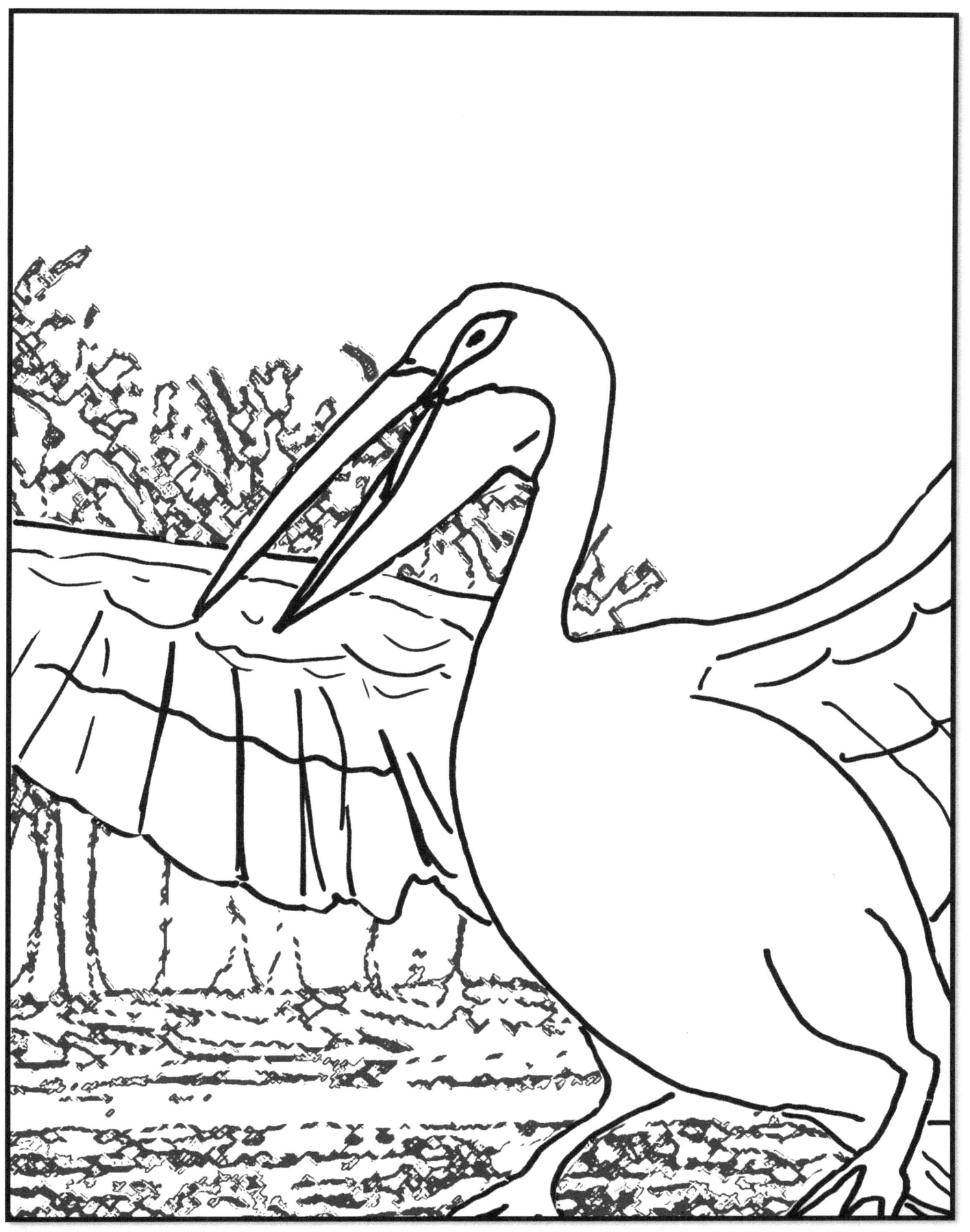

SHEEPSQUATCH

ALSO KNOWN AS THE GOATMAN, THIS SASQUATCH TYPE CREATURE HAS BEEN SEEN IN THE LAST 50 YEARS IN PARTS OF WEST VIRGINIA, PENNSYLVANIA, MARYLAND AND KENTUCKY. THE CREATURE IS VARIOUSLY SIGHTED AS BIPEDAL AND QUADRUPEDAL WHICH MAY HINT AT THERE BEING TWO DIFFERENT ANIMALS IDENTIFIED AS THE SHEEPSQUATCH.

IN THE MID-1970S A CREATURE DESCRIBED AS BEING HALF SHEEP AND HALF MAN TERRORIZED THE WESTERN PENNSYLVANIA TOWN OF WATERFORD. HUNDREDS OF PEOPLE WITNESSED THE CREATURE DESCRIBED AS A LARGE WHITE HAIRED HOOVED BIPED WITH LARGE HORNS AND A SHEEP-LIKE HEAD. IT HARASSED LOCAL FARMERS BY RAIDING HENHOUSES AND EATING ALL THE LIVESTOCK.

DURING THE 1990S A SIMILAR CREATURE WAS SIGHTED IN WEST VIRGINIA, THE MAJORITY OF THE SIGHTINGS TAKING PLACE IN BOONE COUNTY. THIS CREATURE WAS DESCRIBED AS A LARGE WHITE HAIRED QUADRUPED WITH A DOG-LIKE HEAD WITH SMALL HORNS. IT ALSO SPORTED A LONG TAIL. THE CREATURE WOULD OCCASIONALLY STAND ON ITS HIND LEGS AND WHEN IT DID SO, IT WAS ESTIMATED TO BE OVER SIX FEET TALL. THE CREATURE WAS USUALLY PEACEFUL AND SOLITARY, OFTEN FINDING ITS MEALS FROM THE FISH IN LOCAL STREAMS AND CREEKS. BUT ON OCCASION IT WAS REPORTED TO PURSUE THOSE WHO ENCOUNTERED IT IN THE WILD. RECENTLY THERE HAVE BEEN MANY CRYPTID RESEARCHERS WHO HAVE LAUNCHED HUNTING EXPEDITIONS TO FIND THE CREATURE, BUT SO FAR IT HAS BEEN EXTREMELY ELUSIVE.

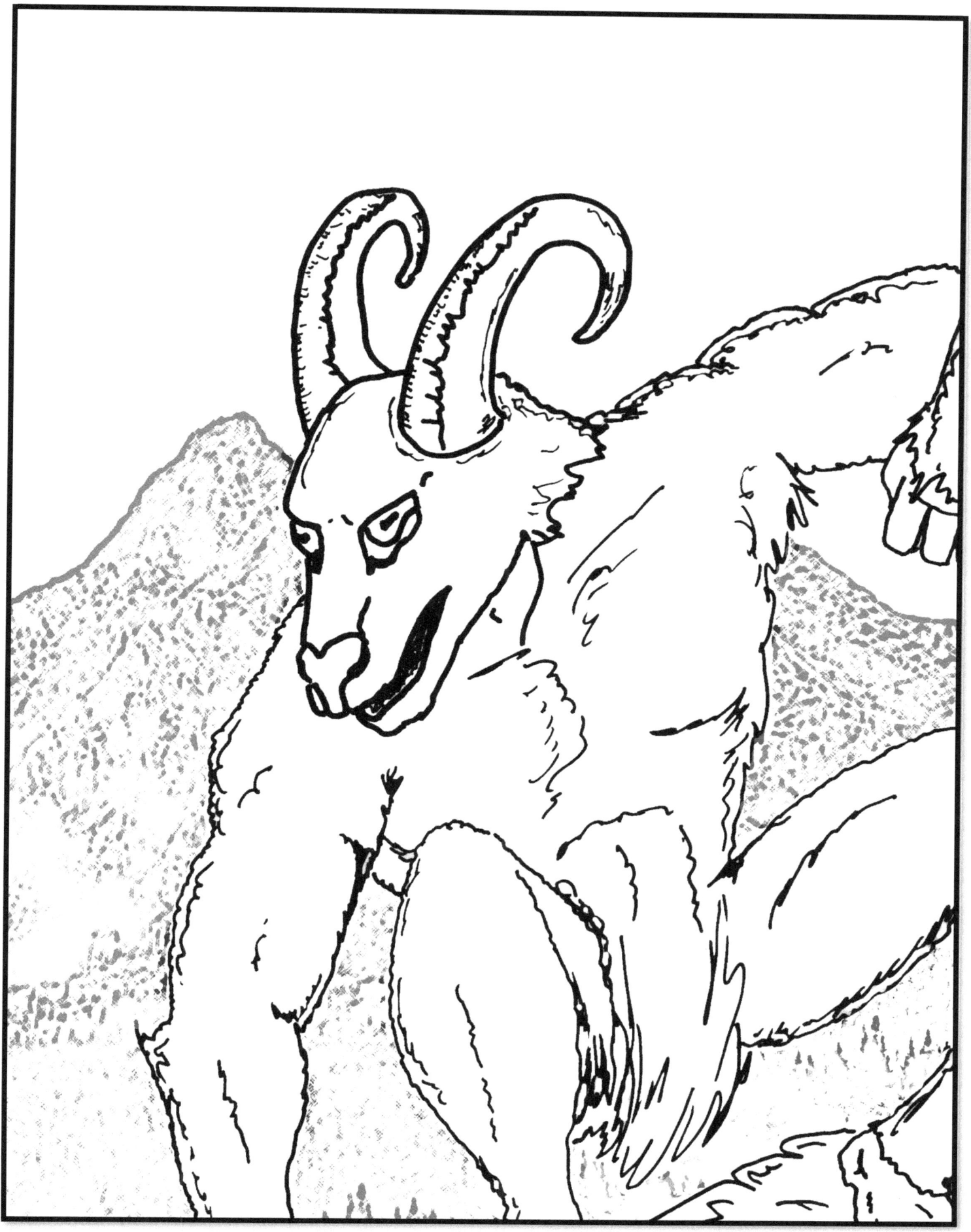

SHEEPSQUATCH

Legends of an unholy hybrid of man with sheep or goats have been a part of the human narrative for many millennia.

One of the earliest recorded appearance of a goat-human hybrid in human history is in Greek mythology. The Satyr was originally portrayed as having horse like features instead of that of a goat or sheep, but in later interpretations their animal features became more goat like. This may be due to a mixing of mythological creatures with the Roman deity Faunus. Faunus was one of the oldest indigenous Roman gods, who was the horned god of the forest, plains and fields. Faunus was worshiped by Rome for many centuries, significantly at the February 15th festival of Lupercalia, where when the Luperci priests wore goat skins and hit onlookers with belts made of goat skin. In essence Faunus (and his female companion Fauna) were manifestation of forest and animal spirits who would aid or harm (depending on their mood and the individual encountered) those who travelled the deep woods. Later Faunus morphed into the god Pan.

Similar creatures appeared in the legends of many European cultures such as the Glaistig of Scotland, the Perchta of the German Alps, the Frau Faste of Switzerland, the Ördög of Hungary and even the Krampus of Celtic Christmas traditions.

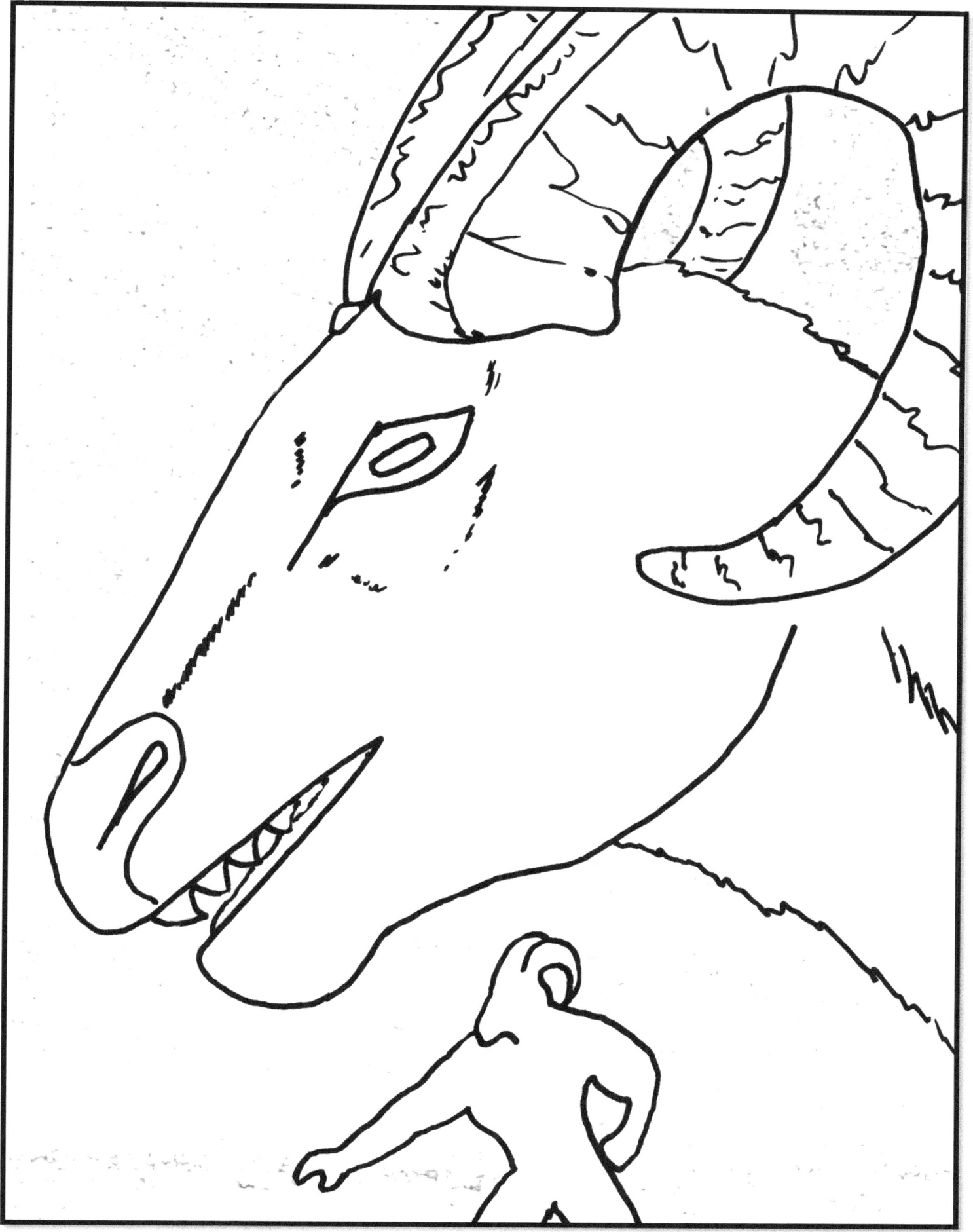

SHEEPSQUATCH

Louisville, Kentucky has a legendary Sheepsquatch creature as well, The Pope Lick Monster of The Louiseville suburb of Fisherville.

The legend of the Pope Lick Monster centers on a Norfolk Southern railroad trestle which passes over Pope Lick Creek in Fisherville. Many variations of the curse of the trestle have been circulated in the local population but since the 1988 film "The Legend of the Pope Lick Monster" focuses on a Sheepsquatch type creature that lures victims onto the trestle and then either attacks them (sometimes with a bloody axe) or pushes them off the 99 foot tall trestle to their death.

The trestle itself is 772 foot long and there is only room for the train itself, so anyone venturing across the trestle would have a hard time making it to safety before being hit and killed by the oncoming locomotive. Many deaths at the trestle have been blamed on the Pope Lick Monster, but actual sightings of a creature have been rare. Although Norfolk Southern has erected an eight foot tall fence to keep unwanted thrill seekers off the tracks, many have died while trying to catch a glimpse of the creature while crossing the trestle. On April 23, 2016 a 26 year old tourist from Dayton on a local ghost hunting tour heard about the Pope Lick Monster and was killed when she could not get off the tracks in time while trying to encounter the creature.

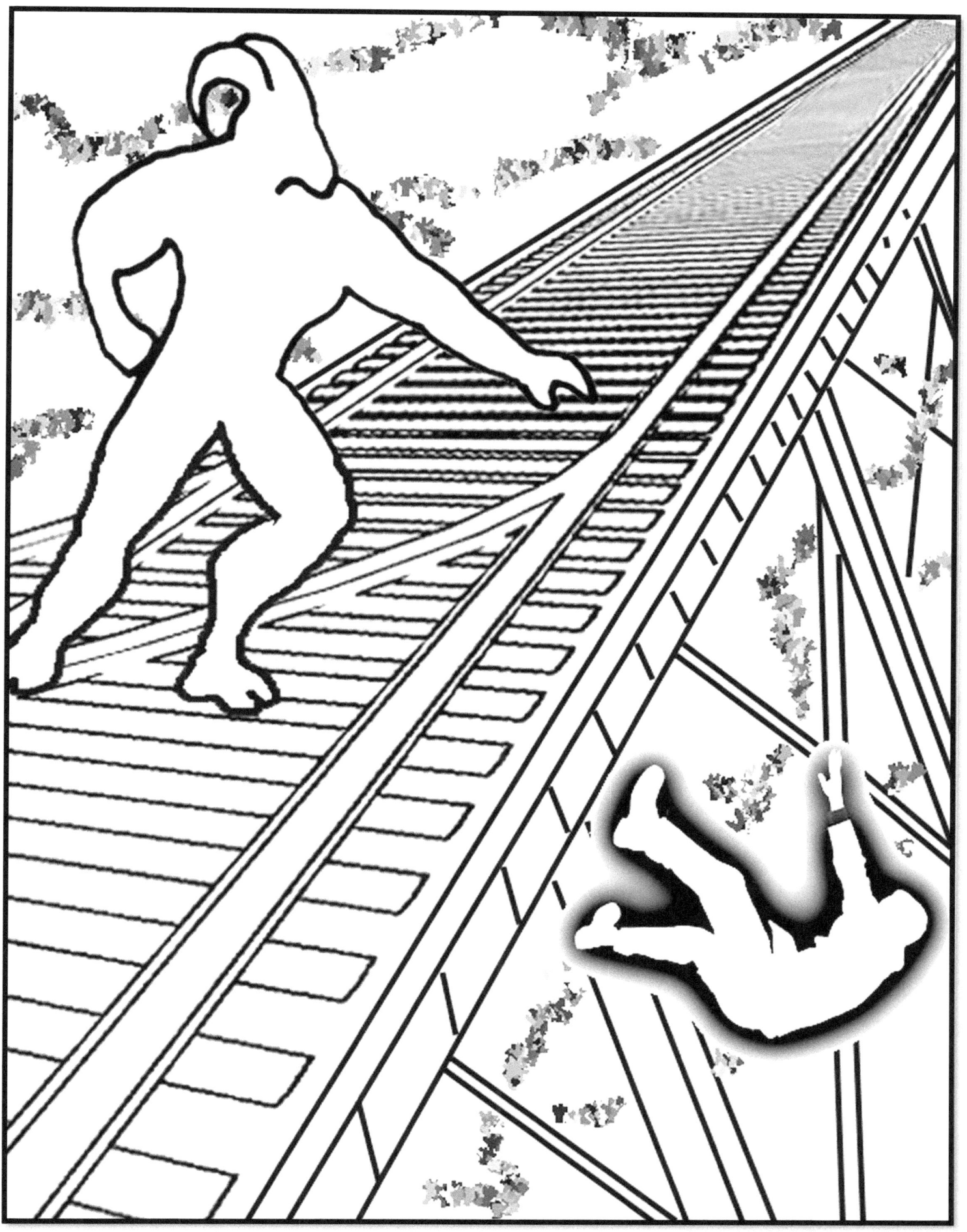

THE DOVER DEMON

On April 21, 1977 an odd and terrifying creature descended upon the streets of Dover Massachusetts and roamed the area for a few days.

At 10:32pm that evening, seventeen year old Bill Bartlett was driving north on Farm street with his friends Mike Mazzocca and Andy Brodie when Bartlett saw something crawling near a broken stone wall on the left side of the road. The creature turned toward the approaching car and its large lidless oval eyes glowed an eerie orange. The creature was no taller than four foot and had a large oversized watermelon shaped head, a body like a baby's, and long thin appendages with large hands and feet covered in glistening peach colored skin. The encounter lasted only a few seconds and neither of Bartlett's companions saw the creature. At midnight that same night fifteen year old John Baxter encountered the creature on Miller Hill road while walking home from his girlfriend's house. He encountered it along the road and assuming it to be a friend in the dark moved to greet it. The creature ran down a path toward a creek where Baxter saw the same creature as Bartlett described standing with its hand "molded" around a rock thirty feet away across a small gully.

The next evening another fifteen year old, Abby Brabham encountered the creature on Springdale Avenue.

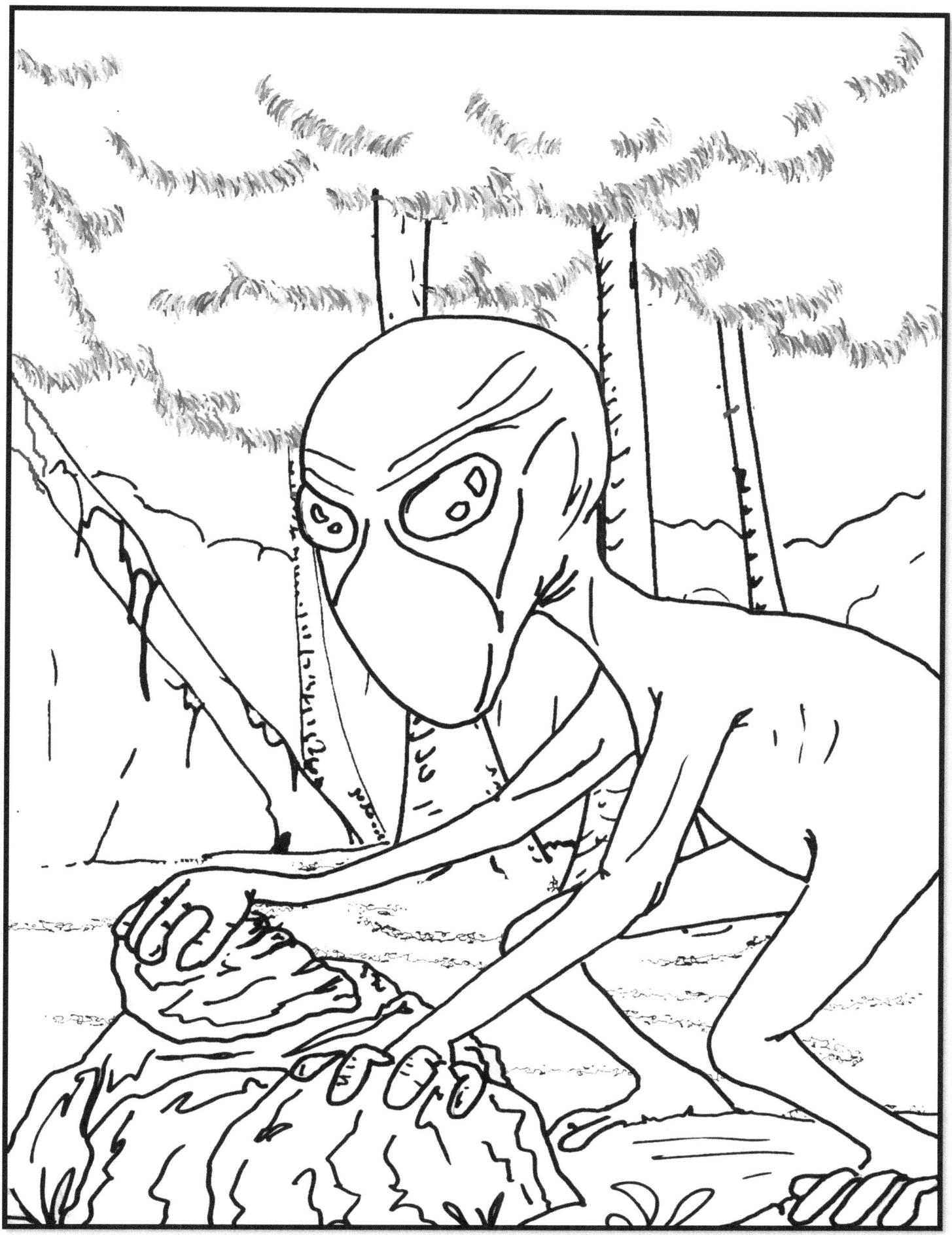

THE DOVER DEMON

AFTER ITS INITIAL APPEARANCES IN 1977, THERE SEEMS TO HAVE BEEN NO OTHER CONFIRMED SIGHTINGS OF THE CREATURE. BUT WHAT EXACTLY DID THESE THREE YOUNG PEOPLE ENCOUNTER ON THOSE TWO DAYS IN APRIL SO MANY YEARS AGO?

WHILE POLICE LATER CLAIMED THE INCIDENTS MAY HAVE BEEN A HOAX, SOME SKEPTICS INITIALLY CLAIMED THAT PERHAPS THE TEENS MISTOOK A LOST BABY CALF OR MOOSE AS THE ODD CREATURE IN THE DARKNESS OF NIGHT.

OTHERS HAVE NOTICED THAT THE DOVER DEMON BEARS AN UNCANNY LIKENESS TO A STEREOTYPICAL GREY ALIEN THAT IS OFTEN ENCOUNTERED WITH UFO LANDINGS OR ALIEN ABDUCTIONS. HOWEVER THE TEENS NEVER ENCOUNTERED A UFO ON THOSE EVENINGS.

OTHERS CLAIM THE DOVER DEMON WAS A MODERN APPEARANCE OF THE LEGENDARY NATIVE AMERICAN CREATURE THE MANNEGISHI. ACCORDING TO NATIVE AMERICAN CREE LORE THE MANNEGISHI WERE A HUMANOID RACE OF TRICKSTERS WHO HAD THIN GANGLY ARMS, SIX FINGERED AND HAD AN OVERSIZED FACE WITH NO NOSE. THEY WERE A LITTLE PEOPLE WHO STRONGLY RESEMBLE THE EUROPEAN LEGENDS OF ELVES IN NOT JUST PHYSICALLY; LIKE EUROPEAN ELVES THE MANNEGISHI WOULD TRICK PEOPLE AND CAUSE HARM OR DEATH. THE DOVER AREA WAS HOME TO MANY NATIVE AMERICAN TRIBES, AND THE PLACES WHERE THE CREATURE WAS SIGHTED WAS ONCE NATIVE LAND.

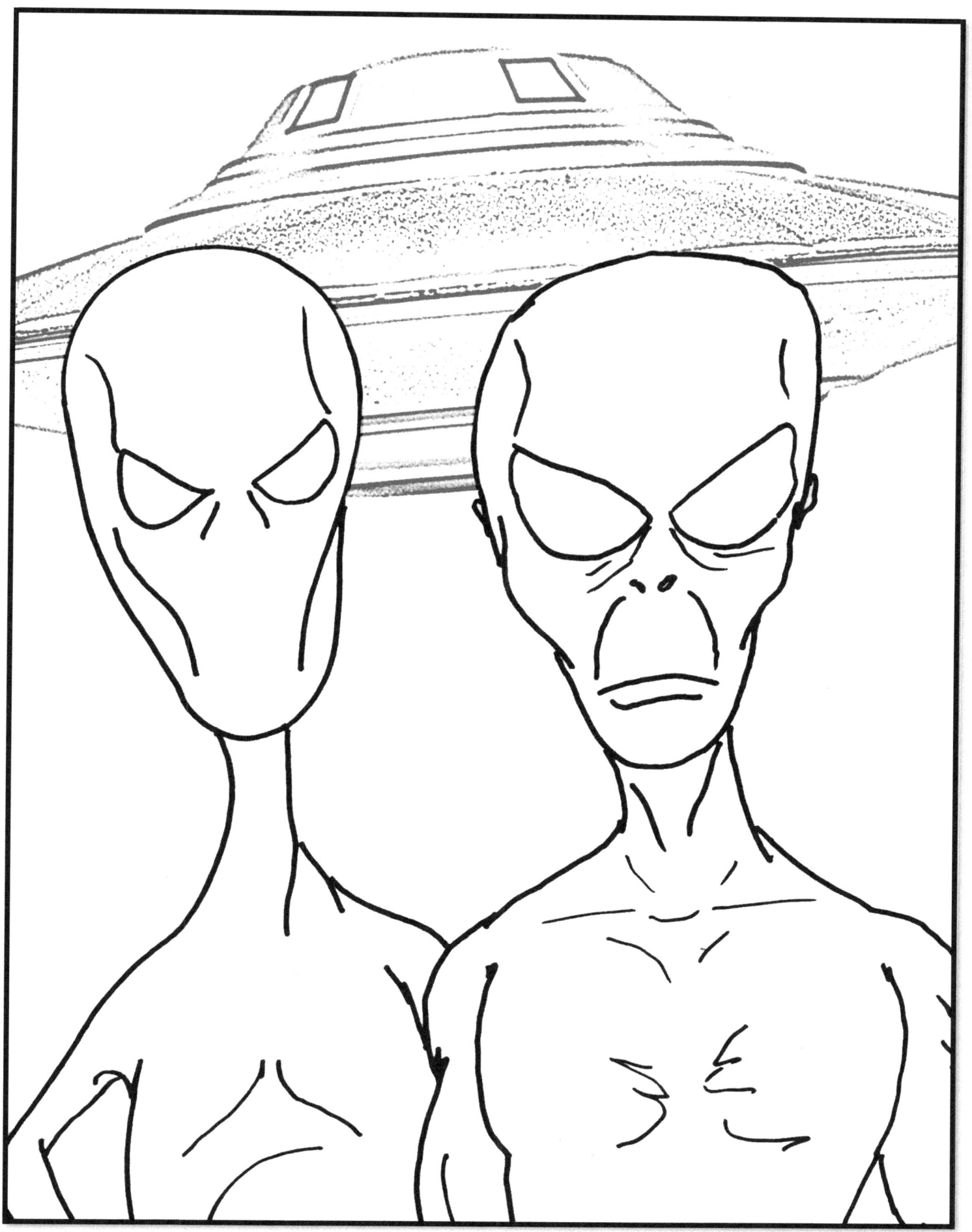

MOTHMAN

On November 15, 1966, couples Roger and Linda Scarberry and Steve and Mary Mallette encountered a large white humanoid figure with glowing red eyes and huge ten foot wings on a road next to a military munitions site near Point Pleasant, West Virginia. The couples claim that the creature followed their car from the air for a period of time. Soon, others encountered this "Mothman", from firefighters to grave diggers. The sightings continued until December 15, 1967, when the collapse of the Silver Bridge killed 46 people, and the sightings ceased. Since then the Mothman has been seen as a harbinger of death and disaster.

The Mothman sightings often were connected with that of UFOs which led many paranormal researchers to claim that the creature was an alien. Author John Keel in his 1975 book "The Mothman Prophecies" claims that witnesses to the creature also had visitations by legendary UFO black operation agents the Men in Black who harassed them in order to change or retract their testimonies of the creature.

The Mothman has so affected the local population of Point Pleasant that since 2002 there has been an annual Mothman Festival on the third weekend of September that has become a tourist attraction.

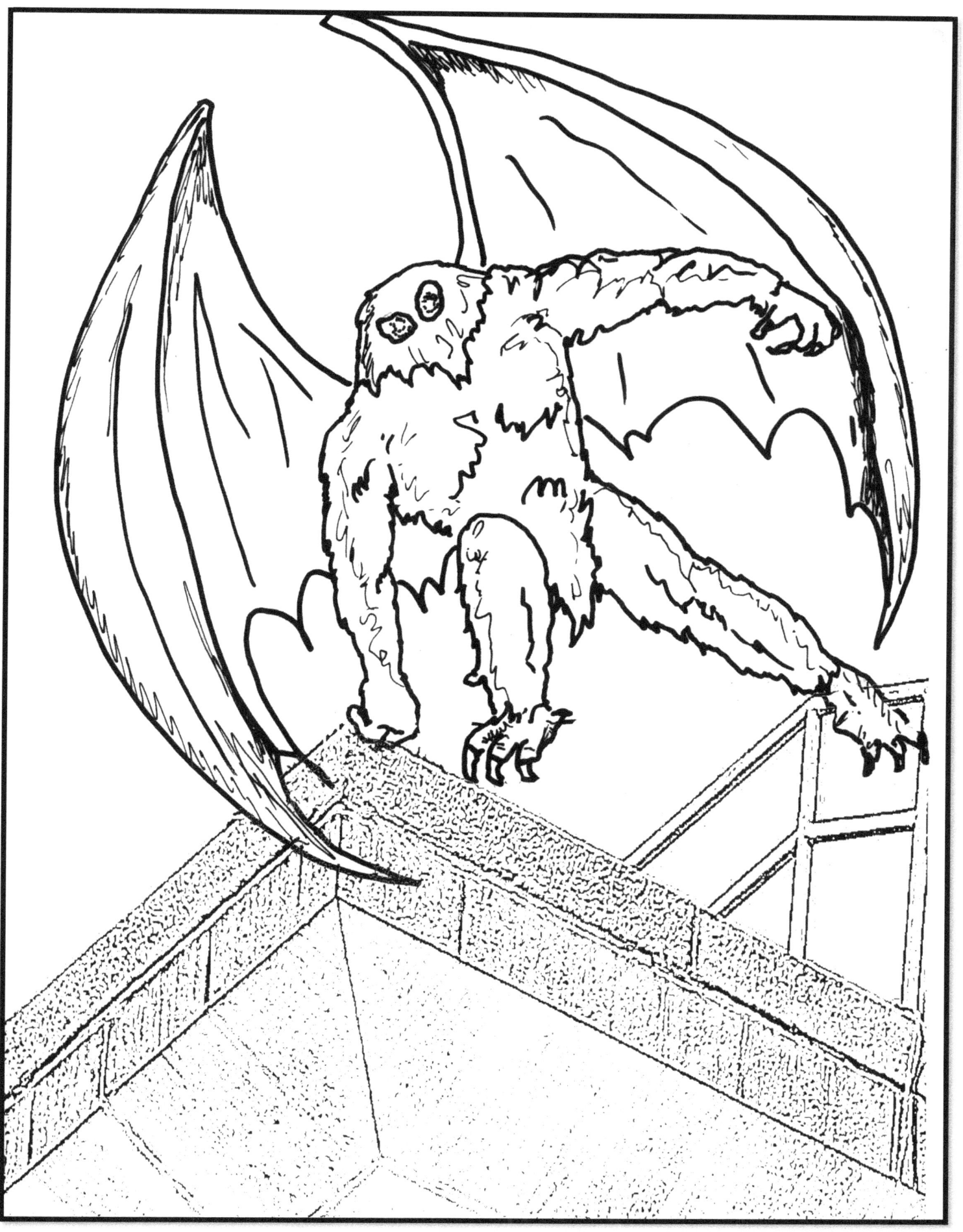

MOTHMAN

The descriptions of Mothman remain constant that it is a flying humanoid being with very large wings and large luminescent eyes. However there has been a variety of differences in its appearance as reported by various witnesses. Some witnesses, especially the in the earliest sightings in 1966-1967 describe the creature as a headless and armless humanoid. The eyes instead of being on a head atop a neck structure from the shoulders are set in the chest area of the creature. Instead of arms, the creature has its two great wings protruding from its shoulders.

Others have seen a more typical humanoid being in their Mothman encounters with a head that is home to the glowing eyes and arms distended from its shoulders as well as wings upon its back. These sightings are usually after 1967 and often not in the area of West Virginia where the original sightings took place. This type of Mothman creature has been sighted in Colorado, Tennessee, Minnesota, New York and other countries such as Russia and Germany. In many cases it also has heralded disaster.

The drawing on the next page is based on the 1966-1967 sightings in West Virginia as envisioned by artist Gene Duplantier.

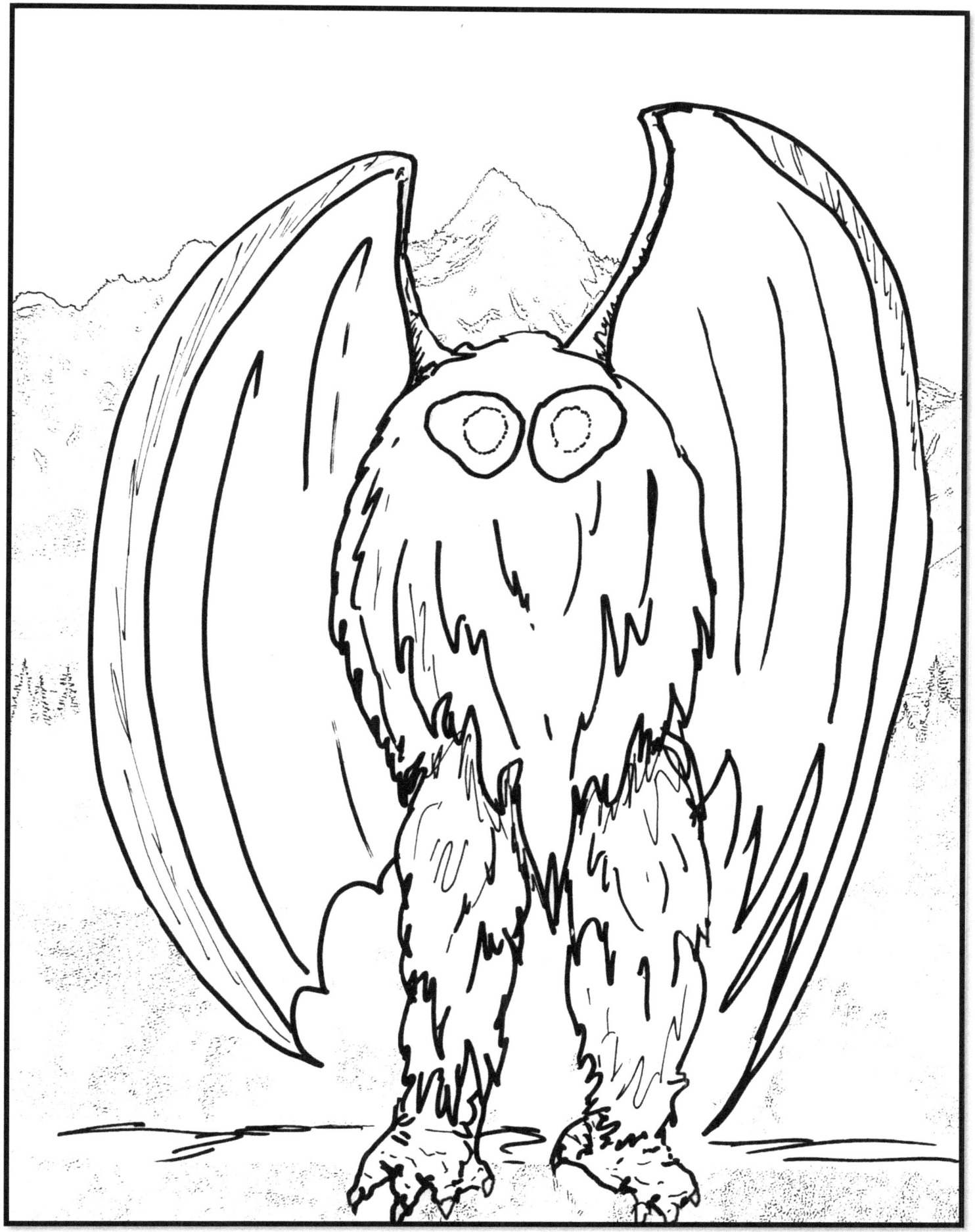

MOTHMAN

SOME OF THE POSSIBLE EXPLANATIONS OF THE MOTHMAN SIGHTINGS IS THAT WITNESSES ARE CONFUSING COMMON ANIMALS OR ANIMALS OUTSIDE OF THEIR NATURAL RANGE AS THE CRYPTID CREATURE.

THE FIRST OF THESE WAS DR. ROBERT L. SMITH, WILDLIFE BIOLOGIST AT WEST VIRGINIA UNIVERSITY. DR. SMITH CLAIMS THAT WITNESSES CONFUSED A SANDHILL CRANE THAT HAD WANDERED OUT OF ITS NATURAL MIGRATION ROUTE WITH THE SUPERNATURAL CREATURE. THE SANDHILL CRANE ROUGHLY FITS THE MOTHMAN DESCRIPTION, IT CAN REACH A HEIGHT OF FOUR FEET WITH A WINGSPAN OF OVER SEVEN FOOT ACROSS. THE SANDHILL CRANE ALSO HAS LARGE RED CIRCLES AROUND ITS EYES.

ANOTHER POPULAR NATURAL IDENTIFICATION FOR THE MOTHMAN SIGHTINGS ARE LARGE OWLS. THE GREAT GREY OWL IS NATIVE TO THE NORTHERN HEMESPHERE AND CAN REACH A HEIGHT OF UP TO THREE FOOT. MALE GREAT GREY OWLS CAN HAVE A WINGSPAN OF UP TO FIVE FEET AND OWLS LIKE OTHER ANIMALS THAT HUNT AT NIGHT HAVE TAPETUM LUCIDUM. TAPETUM LUCIDUM IS A LAYER OF TISSUE IN THE EYE BEHIND THE RETINA THAT REFLECTS BACK THROUGH THE RETINA AND GIVES THE ANIMAL BETTER NIGHT VISION AND AN EERIE GLOW. IN RECENT YEARS MANY ABOVE AVERAGE SIZE OWLS HAVE BEEN SIGHTED IN THE OHIO VALLEY AND SPECIFICALLY AREAS OF WESTERN PENNSYLVANIA AND WEST VIRGINA.

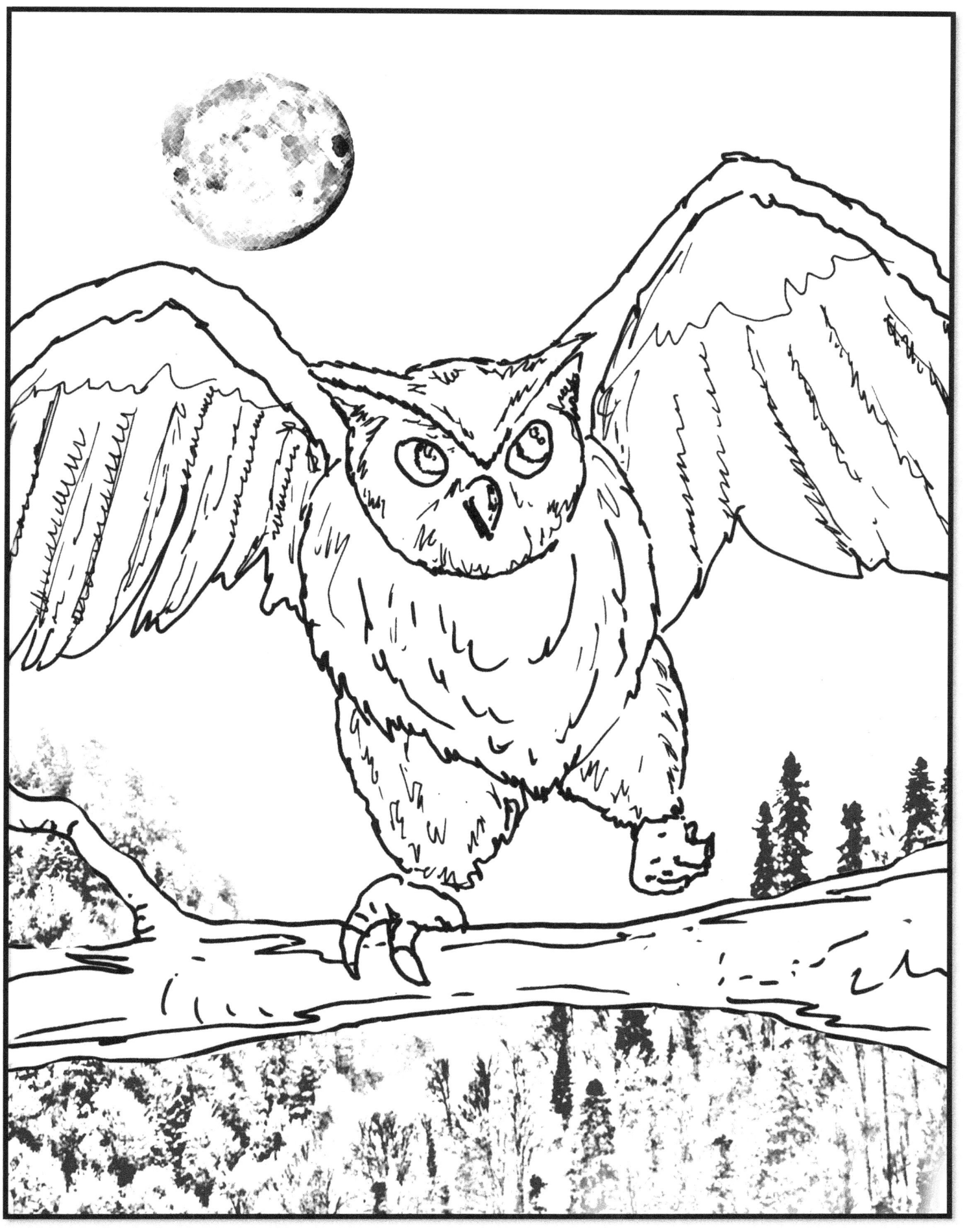

PHANTOM PANTHER

ALSO KNOWN AS ALIEN BIG CATS, THESE ARE LARGE PANTHERS, COUGARS, LIONS OR LEOPARDS SEEN FAR OUTSIDE OF THEIR NATURAL HABITAT. PHANTOM PANTHERS HAVE BEEN ENCOUNTERED ACROSS THE GLOBE, BUT THERE HAS BEEN AN ABUNDANT AMOUNT OF SIGHTINGS IN GREAT BRITAIN, THE UNITED STATES, HAWAII, CANADA, AUSTRALIA, NEW ZEALAND AS WELL AS PARTS OF EUROPE AND RUSSIA. PHANTOM PANTHERS ARE OFTEN SEEN IN SUBURBAN AREAS WERE NO NATIVE LARGE FELINE SPECIES WERE THOUGHT TO EXIST.

SIGHTINGS OF PHANTOM PANTHERS HAVE BEEN EXPLAINED AS ESCAPED CIRCUS ANIMALS OR EXOTIC PETS SINCE THE MID-1800S. THOUGH SOME HAVE PROPOSED THAT THE APPEARANCES OF LARGE FELINES IN UNEXPECTED AREAS ARE EITHER THE REPOPULATION OF ANCIENT HABITATS BY SMALL ELUSIVE SPECIES THAT WERE ONCE THOUGHT TO BE EXTINCT OR A REPOPULATION OF THESE AREAS BY AN EXPANSION OF A TOTALLY DIFFERENT SPECIES MIGRATING OR INTRODUCED FROM OTHER AREAS.

PHANTOM PANTHERS ARE USUALLY DESCRIBED AS LARGER THAN A BIG DOG AND HAVING EITHER AN ENTIRE BLACK OR TAN COAT. THEIR BODY SHAPE IS CONSISTENT WITH A LARGE COUGAR, BUT MANY TIMES WITNESSES DESCRIBE THE FELINE AS LOOKING LIKE A LION, COMPLETE WITH A MANE. SOME LION LIKE PHANTOM PANTHER SIGHTINGS IN THE UNITED STATES HAVE BEEN ATTRIBUTED TO A SURVIVING POPULATION OF THE AMERICAN LION (PANTHERA LEO ATROX) THAT SUPPOSEDLY BECAME EXTINCT OVER 11,000 YEARS AGO.

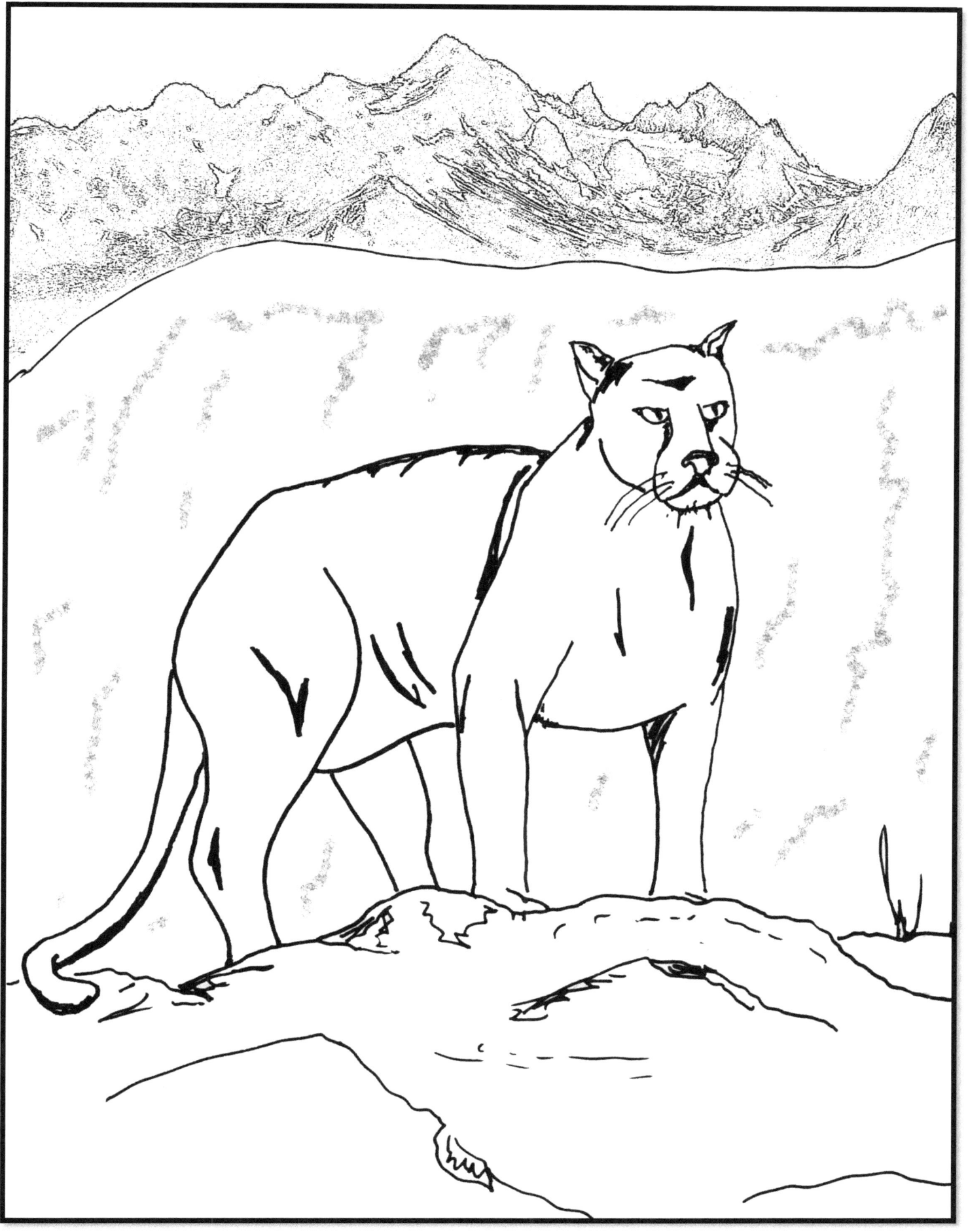

PHANTOM PANTHER

Sometimes Phantom panthers act more phantom-like than panther-like. That is they seem to be some sort of preternatural creature that can appear or disappear at their whim. Witnesses capture a look at the creature and they disappear without a trace and sometimes even without any tracks.

Many indigenous cultures venerated large feline creatures, and many of the modern sightings of Phantom Panthers occur not just in ancient habitats of the animals, but also in former areas of indigenous populations that worshiped the animal. This leads some researchers to speculate that they are the bygone totems of the ancient indigenous religions whose spirit still haunt their native land. Often the witnesses themselves have had ancestors who were part of the native indigenous culture. Perhaps they appear to them as a sign that their power and influence still hold some sway over the area. Or perhaps it is just ancestral memory manifesting itself in what seems to the observer a physical form.

Some paranormal researchers think that rather than being a spirit guide type of totem, the Phantom Panthers being sighted are actually ghosts of the animal. Some point to a residual haunting of some sort where it is a kind of recording playing back events of the past, while others propose that they are sentient spirits who wander their old hunting grounds.

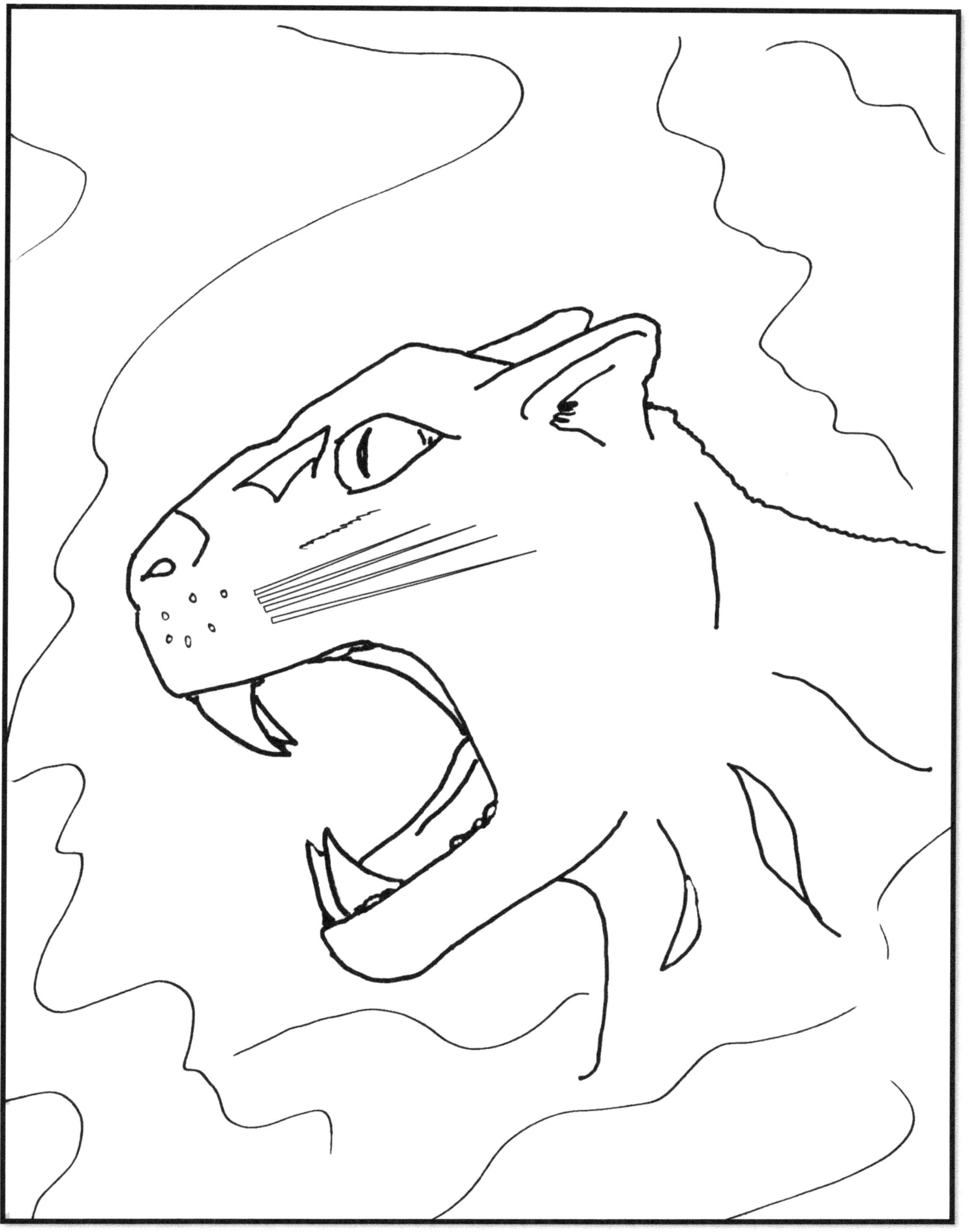

LIZARD MAN

Humanoid Reptilian creatures have long been associated with world myths, but in the past few hundred years various sightings or reptilian creatures have been sighted across the globe.

The most famous of these is the Lizard Man of Scape Ore Swamp, of South Carolina's Lee County. This creature could be called a composite of a Sasquatch like creature and a reptilian humanoid since it is covered with hair and has reptilian hands covered in scales. It was first reported on June 29, 1988 by 17yr old Christopher Davis, who described it as 7 foot tall with glowing red eyes.

Lizard humanoids tend to be dwell close to a natural water resource such as the Thetis Lake Monster whose lake home is Victoria, British Columbia, Canada. On August 22, 1972 two teenagers encountered the reptilian creature which was about 5ft tall and covered with silver scales. Although some have claimed the creature was really a pet Tegu Lizard which a local man had as a pet at the time, police have rejected this theory. Similar creatures have been sighted for decades in waterways and lakes in Delaware, Louisiana, Ohio, and North Carolina in The United States. A similar creature is also part of the spiritual belief system of the Hydah, an indigenous people of the Pacific Northwest Coast of North America and Haida Gwaii Island in northern British Columbia.

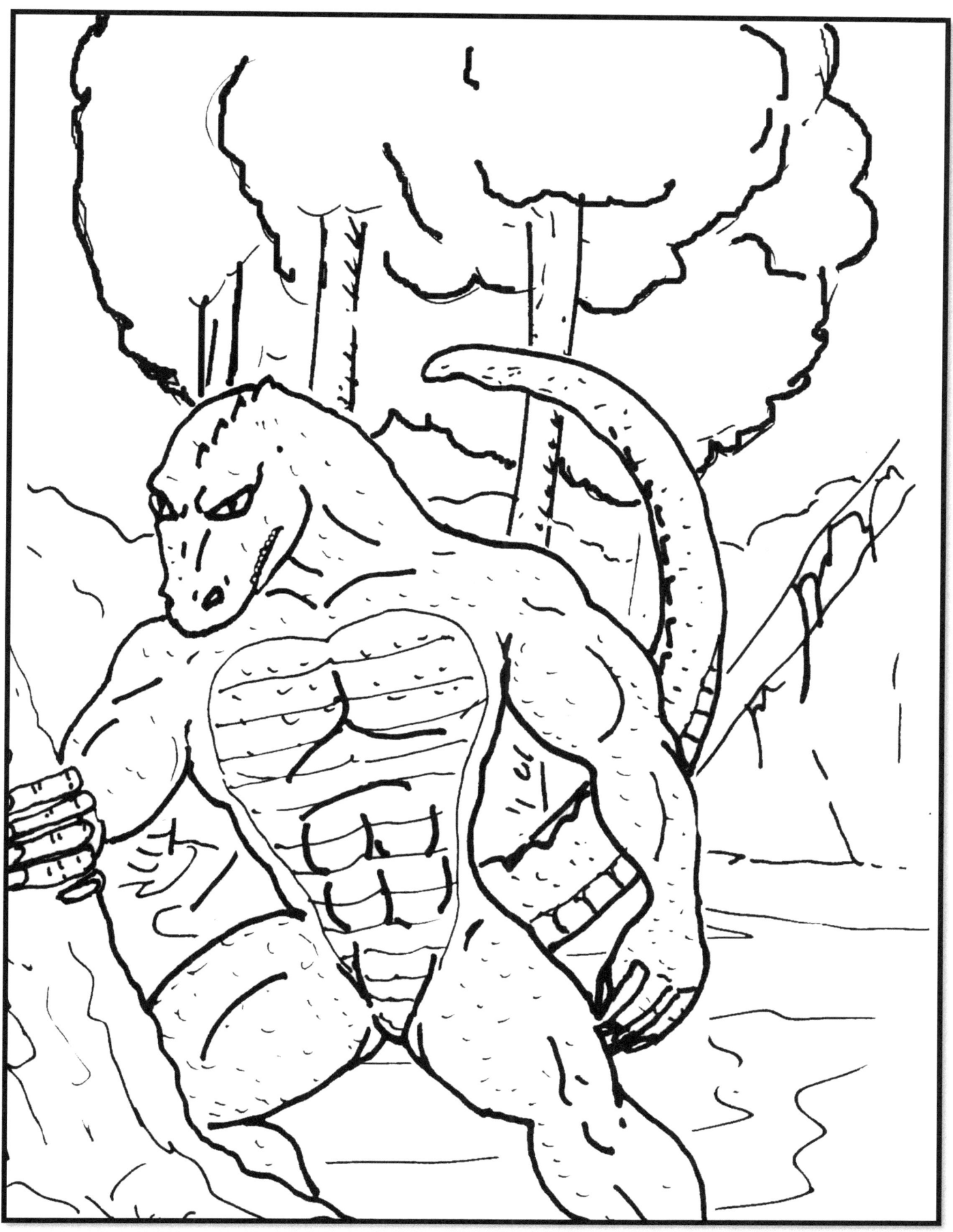

LIZARD MAN

What is Dinosaurs had escaped or survived the Cretaceous-Tertiary extinction event and evolved into an intelligent being? This thought is the basis of a theory of by geologist/palaeontologist Dale Alan Russell of North Carolina State University. In 1982 Russell theorized a possible evolutionary path for the Theropodian Dinosaur Troodon, which had a higher intelligence in comparison to other dinosaurs of its era. If it had survived and evolved, it could have had a superior intelligence which would rival human beings and its frame would evolve into a distinctly humanoid figure. According to Professor Russell, the "Dinosauroid" would have a three fingered hand with an opposable thumb and large oval eyes.

If Professor Russell's theory is correct, perhaps this would explain the numerous reports of reptilian humanoids sightings worldwide as well as the global spanning presence of reptilian humanoids in world mythology.

Having had millions of years advance in evolution to that of human beings, perhaps the Dinosauroids also had an advanced culture and technology. It may be why so many world mythologies like that of ancient Sumeria have tales of reptilian humanoids teaching their ancestors the basics of civilization.

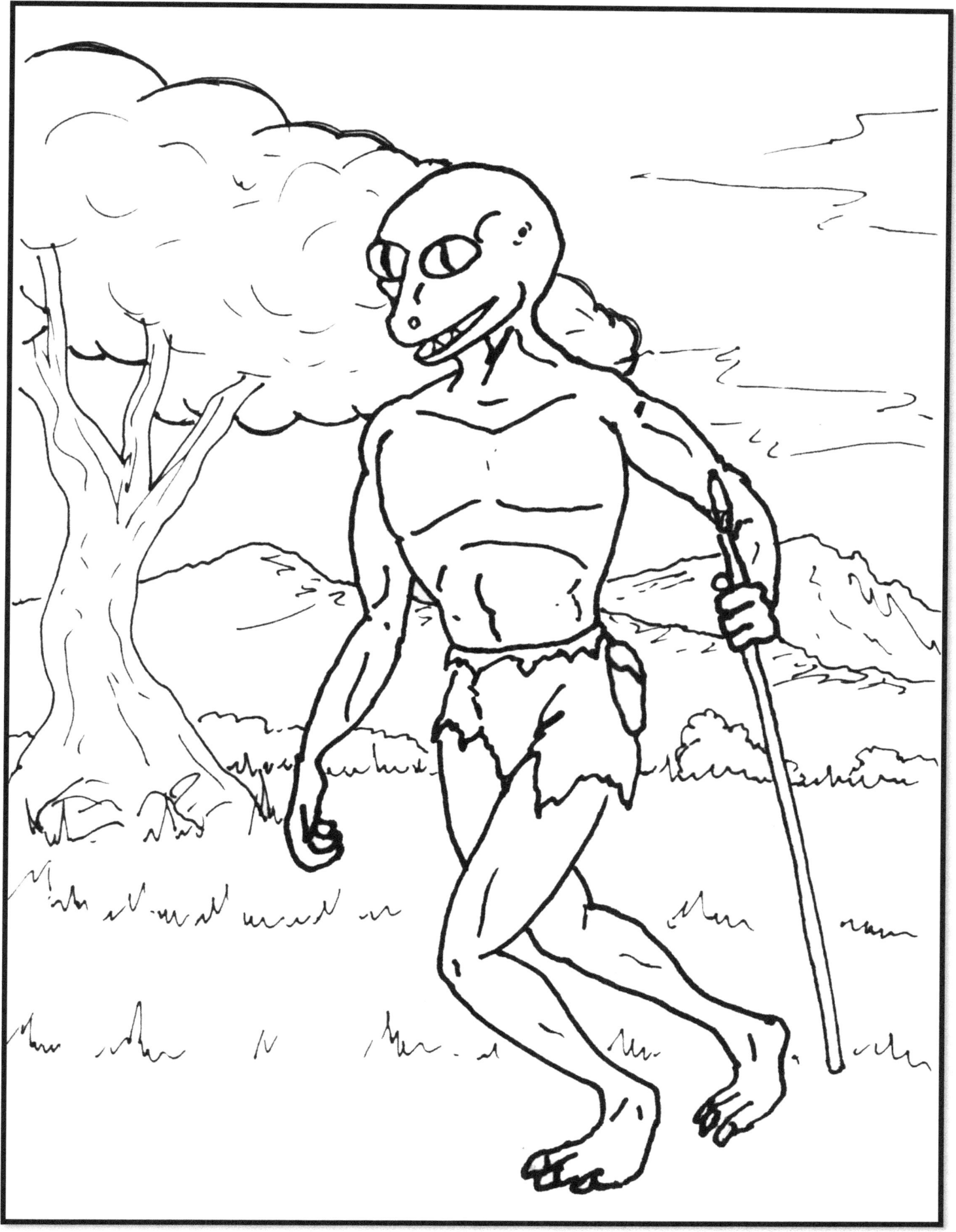

LIZARD MAN

If the Dinosauroids survived the mass extinction at the end of the Cretaceous many researchers believe they might have done so by going underground.

Stories of underground lizard humanoids are not uncommon. In the January 29th 1934 edition of the LA Times the headline read: "Lizard People's Catacomb City Hunted". In the article, reporter Jean Bosquet highlighted the effort of geophysical mining engineer G. Warren Shufelt who was "now engaged in an attempt to wrest from the lost city deep in the earth below Fort Moore Hill the secrets of the Lizard People of legendary fame in the medicine lodges of the American Indian" Shufelt apparently was told of a treasure room by a Hopi Indian chief in Arizona, and the treasure room was supposedly located underneath 2nd Street and Broadway; a map was included in the article.

The Hopi Indians believe they descend from Snake People, and claim through legend that there are Snake People who live in the underworld and who occasionally visited the tribe in the past. This legend is brought to life through the Hopi Snake Dance. Writer David Icke, a modern theorist that Lizardmen now control the world's political system claims the snake People have ancient gold tablets that contain vast amounts of secret knowledge.

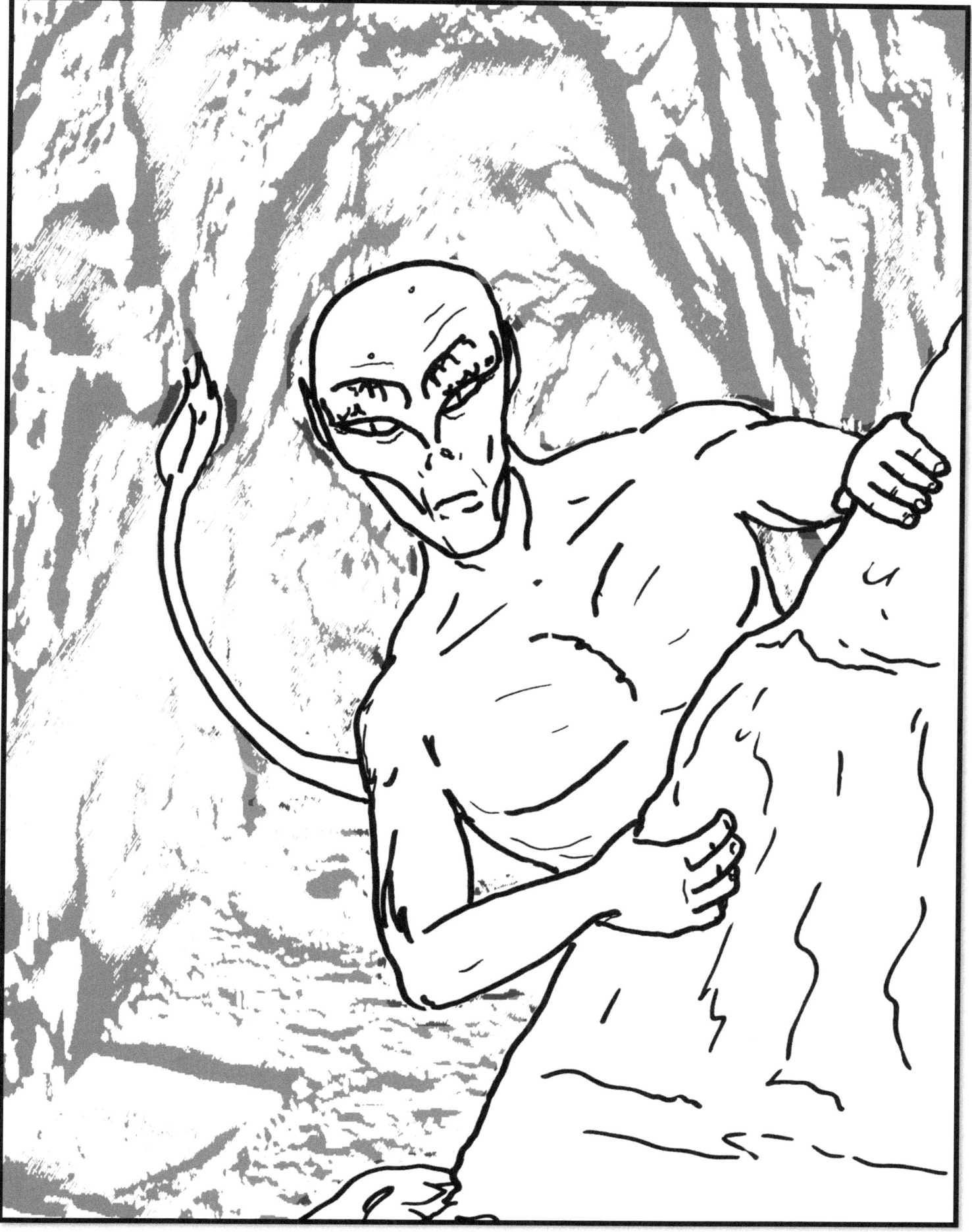